A Paideia Book

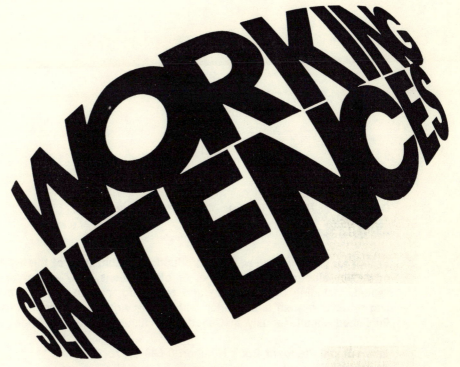

Robert L. Allen
Teachers College, Columbia University

Rita Pompian
Pace University

Doris Allen
Teachers College, Columbia University

Thomas Y. Crowell Company
Established 1834   New York

International Standard Book Number: 0-690-00770-1
Thomas Y. Crowell Company
666 Fifth Avenue
New York, New York 10019
Typography and cover design by Arthur Ritter
Manufactured in the United States of America

ACKNOWLEDGMENTS

Grateful acknowledgment is made to the following authors and publishers for their permission to reprint the following copyrighted material:
G. P. Putnam's Sons for the extract from THE ONCE AND FUTURE KING by T. H. White. Copyright 1939-40 by T. H. White. © 1958 by T. H. White. Reprinted by permission of G. P. Putnam's Sons.

Charles Scribner's Sons for the extract from THE GREAT GATSBY by F. Scott Fitzgerald. Copyright 1925 by Charles Scribner's Sons; renewal 1953 Frances Scott Fitzgerald Lanahan. Reprinted by permission of Charles Scribner's Sons.

George R. Stewart for the extract from STORM. Copyright 1941 Random House, Inc. Reprinted by permission of the author.

Franklin Watts for the extract from ADVERTISING (A First Book) by Richard O. Pompian. Copyright 1970 Franklin Watts, Inc. Reprinted by permission of Franklin Watts, Inc.

Foreword
To the
Instructor

WORKING SENTENCES is intended to provide the student with experience in writing sentences that exhibit the features of edited English. As the term suggests, edited English refers to the kind of standard written English that typically appears in books, periodicals, and newspapers. Although the English that appears in these examples is published, this circumstance is fairly incidental. The real point is that this kind of written English has been *edited*—reflected upon, tinkered with, improved over the writer's first attempts. As the Introduction suggests, the title of this book is intentionally ambiguous. It refers not only to sentences that work—that is, sentences that serve their purpose—but to the process of working sentences to improve their effectiveness. This second sense of *working* suggests the image of a potter or sculptor working his raw material into a desired form. Obviously, it is not absolutely necessary that a native speaker, in order to write well, know the names of the various elements of an English sentence or that he or she have conscious knowledge of the rules according to which these parts can be moved around, combined, or otherwise manipulated. One can write like an angel and yet lack much or any conscious knowledge of the structures he or she uses.

However, a book that sets out to provide a means of teaching students to write cannot responsibly assume that all students will be able to do what some people seem to manage so effortlessly. Mature written sentences are characterized by a heavier load of meaning than spoken sentences, and to succeed in loading sentences to their meaningful capacity, it helps to know something about important sentence elements and how they combine in edited English. It is also a help to both instructor and student to be able to pinpoint the specific cause of an error in writing. The student who finds a sentence marked "awkward" in a paper that is returned to him may or may not be able to find a remedy. Certainly, his chances of improving the sentence are much greater if the instructor can specify the exact nature of the problem and refer the student to earlier discussion of the construction involved.

Sector Analysis, the system of analysis on which WORKING SENTENCES is based, is particularly suitable for the authors' purpose. It differs from most other grammars in two important ways: It is construction-oriented, not word-oriented; and it is a grammar of written English rather than of spoken English.

In sector analysis, the sentence is viewed as consisting of a sequence of positions, called sectors, which may be filled by different kinds of constructions, such as phrases and clauses. Each construction, in turn, consists of a sequence of positions for still other constructions which function on a lower level of structure.

By focusing the student's attention on large constructions rather than on individual words in a sentence, sector analysis helps him or her to recognize these larger units and to grasp their syntactic relationships. Work with large syntactic units leads to the ability to combine related thoughts into a single grammatical and rhetorically effective sentence. In the beginning, students must practice sentence combining consciously as they edit their own writing; but given enough practice, they should in time internalize the skills involved and be able to produce an increasing number of mature sentences in their first drafts.

Under the best of circumstances, it takes time and effort to internalize a writing skill. But the student's task is lightened considerably when he or she uses a grammar that accurately describes the kinds of sentences he or she is expected to write—that is, a grammar of written English. The inexperienced writer tends to write as he or she speaks. The instructor, on the other hand, is likely to judge the student's writing against the standards of edited written English. All too often, the student is unaware of the sentence-combining processes involved in making a first draft into a final draft, with the result that revisions are likely to be limited to mechanical corrections in spelling and punctuation. Students cannot be expected to produce mature sentences unless they know the constructions that characterize them and how those constructions are put together. The grammar in WORKING SENTENCES makes this knowledge available to students, and the exercises are designed to facilitate the transfer of this knowledge to the student's writing.

The organization of WORKING SENTENCES reflects its main purpose. The first five units review the major constructions of written English and their functions; the remaining ten units focus on sentence-combining techniques of high utility in edited English. In preparing the present edition of WORKING SENTENCES, the authors have benefited greatly from their own experience and the experience of other instructors and students with the preliminary edition of this book, which in one form or another has been in use for more than two years.

CONTENTS

Introduction

The title of this book is intentionally ambiguous. One of its two meanings is more obvious than the other: *Working* sentences are obviously sentences that are productive and businesslike—sentences that do their job. But there is also another meaning for *working:* Potters work clay into pots and vases, and glassblowers work glass into different shapes for different purposes. *Work,* in this sense, means "to shape" or "to form" for a special purpose. What you will be doing as you use this book is working sentences —shaping and molding them to suit your purposes.

You will be dealing mainly with written sentences. In English, as in many modern languages, writing is a separate system—related to, but different from, the system of the spoken language. Some of the differences are quite obvious: There is nothing in spoken English that corresponds to the way a writer indents to show the beginning of a paragraph; nor is there a signal in spoken English that corresponds to the use of capital letters in writing. There are subtler differences as well: Most people use some words in writing that they rarely use in conversation; they also form sentences when they are writing that they would be unlikely to use in speaking. Of course, most spoken sentences can be written down, and most written sentences can be read aloud. The two systems are closely related. But written English has its own special conventions—or rules—which good writers generally try to observe. One important goal of this book is to make clear what these conventions are.

The fact that written language and spoken language are closely related can sometimes create problems. If you have ever tried to learn another language, you have probably had to struggle against your inclination to put the words of that language in the order that you would put them in in English. What you were trying to do was impose upon the new language the conventions of your own; that is, your knowledge of your first language *interfered* with your mastery of the second language. For much the same reason, native speakers of English often have trouble learning to write good English. Their spoken language, which they learned first, interferes with their mastery of written English. For instance, in speech, no one—not even an English professor—uses complete sentences all the time. Conversation is full of unfinished sentences, sentences that run together, and sentences that start one way and end another; in addition, speakers do not always worry about making sure that the forms of the verbs they use match their subjects. All these features, rarely noticed in spoken language, violate conventions of written English.

One assumption that underlies the conventions of written English is that writers have more opportunity than speakers to reflect on their use of language. A speaker has to get his words out as best he can; if he reflects very long on how he is going to say something, he may never have a chance to say it at all. A writer may be in a hurry, too. But unless he is jotting down words for himself only—as on a shopping list or a memo pad—he usually cannot get away with slighting the conventions of writing. Even though it may be produced in haste, late at night, or under distracting conditions, writing is expected to exhibit signs of care and reflection.

The kind of writing you read in magazines, books, and newspapers and the kind that you are expected to use in reports and themes can be called **edited English.** As the term suggests, this is the kind of English that the writer has had the time to go back over and check, or edit, in order to make sure that the conventions of writing have been observed. Only a few lucky people write anything like edited English the first time they start jotting their ideas down on paper. Edited English is usually the result of experimenting with different words and different ways of putting them together. In other words, a writer produces edited English by working his sentences as a potter works his clay. If he is successful, the result will not merely be sentences that are complete and have verbs agreeing with their subjects; the result will be sentences that are more interesting, more effective, and more tightly knit together.

That *tightly knit* in the last sentence is worth thinking about. The ideas in edited English are usually more closely related than those in spoken language, and the sentences that express them are usually packed with more meaning. A speaker usually utters his thoughts as they come to him, often in loose, fairly unconnected sentences. By contrast, an important part of the process of editing is cutting away unnecessary words and finding ways to make the meaning as clear as possible.

As you gain experience in editing your own English, you will learn some new names for the basic units (or "building blocks") from which sentences are made, and you will learn to find the positions in sentences in which these units can be used. Knowing the names for units and positions enables you to talk about sentences. (Unless you know the names of the parts, your instructor cannot tell you the one thing that may be wrong with a sentence that is mostly right.) Knowing the positions in a sentence and the units that can fill them enables you to combine and switch around sentence elements into new and more effective combinations. (As an important fringe benefit, you will find that being able to cut sentences up into their parts will help you to unpack the meaning in the complicated sentences you encounter in your reading.)

The basic procedure in each unit will be the same: You will begin with brief explanations intended to acquaint you with, or remind you of, the important parts of sentences and their functions. From there, you will move on to a set of tasks in which you begin working with other people's sentences and gradually move toward working with sentences you write yourself. The idea behind this progression is simple. The important thing is the sentences *you* write; but since you are not the first to face a blank sheet of paper with a lot of good but elusive ideas in your head, the chances are that you can learn something from the way in which other writers have solved writing problems.

It would be pleasant to think that there is nothing more to writing well than following Sir Philip Sidney's advice: "Look into your heart and write." Undoubtedly, that is good counsel as far as *what* you write is concerned. But *how* you write it—how you form sentences that say what you have to say clearly and effectively—is important, too.

That is really what this book is about. At first, the talk about new terms, sentence units, and sentence positions may sound complicated. You will find that it really is not. In fact, you will discover in the first unit that a simple game you have probably known from childhood provides the key for finding the main positions in a sentence and identifying the units that can fill them. The game is Twenty Questions, and you will soon see that there is more to be learned by asking questions than merely the answers to them.

X-Words

1.1 X-Words and Subjects

Have you ever played Twenty Questions? If you have, you know that one player thinks of something and the others try to guess what it is. The players don't start out by trying to guess the name of the thing right away. Instead of asking "Is it a hippopotamus?" skillful players ask questions that will narrow the possibilities to just a few. For instance, they might ask questions like these:

Is it bigger than a breadbox?

Are there any in this room?

Can it fly?

Will it fit in your pocket?

The player who first thought of the thing to be guessed answers *yes* or *no* to the questions until the others either guess what it is or run out of questions.

Notice that all the questions above *can* be answered with *yes* or *no*. For this reason, questions like these are called **yes-no questions.** Notice that each yes-no question begins with a little word like *is, are, can,* or *will.* These are members of a small set of words called **X-words.** (The most important X-words are printed inside the back cover.) X-words are useful when you are playing Twenty Questions or whenever you need to ask a yes-no question. But X-words can be useful in other ways as well. For instance, by knowing about X-words and about how they behave, you can find the subject of a sentence very easily.

For every yes-no question there is a corresponding **statement.** To find the subject by using X-words, all you have to do is to compare the statement and the question:

> It is bigger than a breadbox.   (statement)
>
> Is it   bigger than a breadbox? (yes-no question)
>
> It is an animal.   (statement)
>
> Is it   an animal? (yes-no question)

As you can see, the statement becomes a question when the X-word *is* is moved to the front of the sentence. It seems, then, that there are two possible positions for an X-word: the position it has in statements (which we will mark **X**) and the position it has in yes-no questions (which we will mark **X̃**). Here is an example with the X-word *am* in it:

> X̃   X
>
> ∨ I am talking loud enough.
>
> Am I   talking loud enough?

Once you have identified the two X positions in any sentence, you can find the subject of that sentence. The **subject** will always consist of the words that come between the two X positions. The subject may be only one word, as in the examples above, or it may consist of many words. For example:

> X̃   *Subject*   X
>
> That snake with the black, red, and yellow stripes is deadly.
>
> Is that snake with the black, red, and yellow stripes   deadly?

We will call the place where the subject goes the **S position,** and we will mark the subject by drawing a rectangle around all the words that fill this position:

> X̃   X
>
> That snake with the black, red, and yellow stripes is deadly.
>
> Is that snake with the black, red, and yellow stripes   deadly?

You should note one more thing. The X-words *am, is,* and *are* are used with different subjects:

am is used only with the subject *I*;

is is used with a subject that names one thing or one person, or when the subject is *it*, *he*, or *she*;

are is used with all other kinds of subjects.

PRACTICE 1

Write each of the following sentences as a yes-no question in the space provided below it. Mark the X and X̃ (shifted X) positions in each sentence (but mark them *above* the *original* sentence); then, in the original sentence, draw a rectangle around all the words between the two X positions and mark the rectangle *S* for *Subject*. (The first one has been done for you.)

    X̃   S   X

1. [Charlie] is always talking on the phone.

    Is Charlie   always talking on the phone?

2. A coral snake is marked with black, red, and yellow stripes.

3. I am doing this problem right.

4. Sword-swallowing is a difficult art to learn.

5. The books on this shelf are on reserve.

6. The bank officers are uncertain as to the whereabouts of the chief teller.

7. The South American travel brochures in his desk are the only clue.

3

1.2 Negative Sentences

If you have looked at the X-words inside the back cover, you know that the words *can, may, will, must,* and *would* are in the list along with *am, is,* and *are.* The other X-words work in exactly the same way as these three. They appear in the X position in statements and in the shifted X position (X̃) in yes-no questions:

      X̃   X

          You can park there all night.

     Can you   park there all night?

     X̃   X

        Arlene would like that movie.

  Would Arlene   like that movie?

As with the X-words *am, is,* and *are,* the two possible positions for these X-words in a sentence enable us to find the subject of the sentence. The subject is whatever comes between the X̃ and the X positions. We will continue to mark the subject with a rectangle and to label it S:

     X̃   X

       That knot will hold.

           S

Will [that knot]   hold?

Every sentence that makes a positive statement has a matching form that makes a **negative** statement. For example:

You can park there all night.

You can't park there all night.

Arlene has seen that movie.

Arlene has not seen that movie.

Sentences are usually made negative by adding *not* or *-n't.* Most of the X-words printed inside the back cover have a negative form that ends with

-n't, a contraction for *not* that has been built into the X-word. The negative form of an X-word is moved up to the front of a sentence to make a yes-no question, just like the plain form:

$$\tilde{X} \qquad X$$

🗸 You can't park there all night.

Can't you   park there all night?

If *not* is used instead of the negative form of the X-word, only the X-word moves up front; the *not* stays behind:

$$\tilde{X} \qquad X$$

You didn't think of it.

Didn't you   think of it?

But—

$$\tilde{X} \qquad X$$

You did not think of it.

Did you   not think of it?

Not has a more formal sound than the negative form of an X-word, and for this reason some people prefer it in edited English. In speaking, however, most people use the negative forms of the X-words.

PRACTICE 2

Fill in an appropriate X-word in the space provided in each of the following statements. Then rewrite each sentence, making it negative by adding *not* after the X-word. (Do not use contractions like *isn't* and *don't* this time.) Mark the X and $\tilde{X}$ positions *in the negative sentence;* then draw a rectangle around the subject and mark it S. (The first one has been done for you.)

1. My friend <u>is</u> studying to be a teacher.
$$\tilde{X} \quad\; S \quad\;\; X$$
   [My friend] is not studying to be a teacher.

2. Some people _____ read Chinese.

3. The team _____ get better as the season goes on.

_____

4. Joanna _____ looking for a full-time job.

_____

5. You _____ help him with his math.

_____

6. Albert _____ go to law school next year.

_____

1.3   Hidden X-Words

So far, we have been making yes-no questions from statements like this one:

X̃   X

He can't hear you.

We simply move the X-word (this time in its negative form) up front, and then we have this yes-no question:

X̃   X

Can't he   hear you?

But how do you make a yes-no question out of a sentence like this next one?

The fans want action.

Want is not an X-word, and we cannot move it up to the front of the sentence:

*Want the fans[1]   action?

---

[1] Asterisks are used to mark sentences that just aren't natural English.

But as you have seen, there has to be an X-word in the X̃ position in every yes-no question. If a statement doesn't already have an X-word in it, we have to put one in before we can change the statement into a yes-no question. What we put in is some form of the X-word *do:*

          do
The fans ∧ want action.

Now that we have an X-word in the X position, we can make a yes-no question as before:

   X̃   X

    The fans do want action.

Do the fans   want action?

Do is one of the X-words that has different forms to match the subject. In the example above, this presents no problem, since *do* is the form that goes with the subject *the fans.* But notice what happens in this example:

That man looks familiar.

         X

       does
That man ∧ look*s̸* familiar.

Does is the form of *do* that is used with subjects like *that man* and *it* and *he* and *she.* When you put *does* into a sentence, you have to drop the *-s* ending from the verb that follows it. If you like, you can think of the *-s* ending as jumping from the verb to the *do:*

That man does look familiar.

(If you want to think of the *-s* as jumping like that, don't worry about where the *e* in *does* comes from. It's just part of the way we spell that word.)

When the statement is changed into a yes-no question, the X-word *does* moves to the X̃ position before the subject:

   X̃   S   X

Does that man   look familiar?

7

PRACTICE 3

Make yes-no questions out of these statements. Since the statements do not contain X-words, you will have to insert a form of *do* in the X position in each sentence. You can do this on the line just below the statement. If you insert the form *does* or *doesn't,* be sure to remove the *-s* from the verb that follows. Then write the yes-no question on the bottom line. (The first one has been done for you.)

1. That looks right.

   That does look right.

   Does that look right?

2. All of these people live here.

3. Everybody likes pizza.

4. The office closes at five.

5. Penny writes a column for the paper.

6. One gallon equals eight pints.

7. The days grow short when you reach September.

1.4 More About Hidden X-Words

As you have seen, one of the most important uses of X-words (in edited English) is for changing statements into yes-no questions by moving the X-word to the $\tilde{X}$ position before the subject. For example:

	X
The first letter of the first word in the title of that book on the table in the corner of the room	is *M.*

$\tilde{X}$ S

Is │the first letter of the first word in the title of that book on the table in the corner of the room │   *M?*

When there is no X-word in the statement, we have to put in some form of *do* (in the X position); we can then move this X-word to the $\tilde{X}$ position to make the yes-no question. For example:

	X
The first word in the title of that book on the table in the corner of the room	begins with *M.*

The first word in the title of that book on the table in the corner of the room	does begin with *M.*

$\tilde{X}$ S   X

Does │the first word in the title of that book on the table in the corner of the room │   begin with *M?*

Another important use of X-words is to "carry" the negative marker *-n't* (or *not*) in negative sentences. As you have seen, we can make a sentence negative by adding either *-n't* to the X-word or *not,* as a separate word, after the X-word. In either case, there must be an X-word present to "carry" the negative marker. For example:

           X

My father can   understand Italian.

My father can't   understand Italian.

or: My father cannot[1] understand Italian.

---

[1] *Can* and *not* are often written together as one word: *cannot.*

When there is no X-word in a sentence that we want to make negative, we have to put in some form of *do* (in either the X or the X̃ position) to carry the negative marker. For example:

	X	
My father		knows Italian.
My father	does	know Italian.
My father	doesn't	know Italian.

or: My father does not know Italian.

A third use of X-words is to carry *stress* when we want to make a sentence **emphatic.** In speech we make a sentence emphatic by stressing or accentuating the X-word; in writing we often show the emphasis by underlining the X-word. For example:

I'm studying Hebrew.

I <u>am</u> studying Hebrew.

When there is no X-word in a sentence that we want to make emphatic in this way, we have to put in some form of *do* (in the X position) to carry the stress. For example:

X				X		
I	know Greek.			My sister		knows Greek.
I <u>do</u>	know Greek.			My sister	<u>does</u>	know Greek.

PRACTICE 4

Make each of the following sentences negative by adding either *-n't* or *not* to the X-word. If there is no X-word in a sentence, you will have to put in some form of *do* to add the *-n't* to. (The first two sentences have been done for you.)

1. The Greenbergs live in New York.

   The Greenbergs don't live in New York. _____

2. They are American citizens.

   They aren't American citizens. _____

3. Mr. Greenberg works in Manhattan.

_____

4. His daughter goes to a high school near their home.

_____

5. She is planning to enter college next year.

_____

6. She knows what kind of job she would like to get.

_____

7. Her brother wants to be a teacher.

_____

8. He is very bright.

_____

TASK A

Your basic job is to change all of the statements that follow into yes-no questions. In about half the cases, however, you will be asked to make some change in the statement before you write the question. When you receive instructions like that, carry them out on the first blank line and write the yes-no question on the second. (If there are no special instructions, only one line is provided.) When you have finished rewriting each statement, draw a rectangle around the subject and label it S. (The first one has been done for you.)

1.   S
                              [The store] opens at nine-thirty.

                                                   S
(Rewrite, adding *do* or *does*.)   [The store] does open at nine-thirty.

                                                   S
(Change to yes-no question.)   Does [the store] open at nine-thirty?

2.   The fox can be trusted.

(Use negative form of X-word.)   _____

(Change to yes-no question.)   _____

11

3.   His sister is a movie star.

(Change to yes-no question.)   _____

4.   One of the girls is from Japan.

(Change to yes-no question.)   _____

5.   The last bus leaves at midnight.

(Rewrite, adding *do* or *does*.)   _____

(Change to yes-no question.)   _____

6.   You are going out with Albert.

(Use negative form of X-word.)   _____

(Change to yes-no question.)   _____

7.   Mr. Brown is still Chief Teller.

(Change to yes-no question.)   _____

8.   He was last seen in Brazil.

(Use negative form of X-word.)   _____

(Change to yes-no question.)   _____

TASK B

On the blank lines below, write yes-no questions for each of the answers given. Begin each question with the same X-word that appears in the answer. *NOTE:* If the word *you* is part of the answer, use *I* in your question. (The first one has been done for you.)

1. Can Juan speak Spanish?   Yes, he can.

2. _____   No, they can't.

3. _____   Yes, she will.

4. _____   No, you aren't.

5. _____   Yes, they have.

6. _____ No, we won't.

7. _____ Yes, you can.

8. _____ No, he couldn't.

9. _____ Yes, you are.

10. _____ No, she hasn't.

11. _____ Yes, it does.

12. _____ No, they don't.

13. _____ Yes, you are.

14. _____ Yes, they are.

15. _____ No, he doesn't.

TASK C

Read the following paragraph all the way through. Then go back over it marking the X positions in each sentence; draw a rectangle around each subject, and mark it S. (The first sentence has been done for you.)

X̃   S   X

[Research scientists] have studied the human brain for many years. These

scientists don't always agree about how the brain works. Some facts are

agreed upon, however. There are two sides to the brain. The two sides are

similar in appearance. Each side is used for different functions. Most people

will use the left side of their brains for language. These same people will

use the other side of their brains for doing nonverbal tasks. Some people's

brains may function the other way around. One side of the brain can some-

times perform all of the functions if the other side is damaged. Scientists

don't know exactly how this happens. They do know that the human brain

is a very complex organ.

TASK D

Write seven or eight sentences describing, as concretely and specifically as possible, a single object such as a leaf, a flower blossom, a hamburger, an alarm clock, or the like. Use as many of the five senses as you can in your description: Tell as far as possible what the object looks like, how it smells, how it tastes, how it sounds, how it feels. *Be sure to use an X-word in each of your sentences.* Write all of your sentences in the form of a single paragraph, and make up a title for your paragraph. (The name of the object which you have chosen to describe could serve as the title.)

More About Subjects

2.1 Singular and Plural

As you have seen, the subject of a sentence consists of all of the words that come between the two X positions in the sentence. A subject may consist of just one word, or it may be quite long:

$\tilde{X}$ S   X

    Dogs aren't allowed in this store.

        S

Aren't dogs   allowed in this store?

$\tilde{X}$ S   X

    The person who parked his car in left field must report to the security guard.

Must the person who parked his car in left field report to the security guard?

There are two kinds of subjects in English: **singular subjects** and **plural subjects.** A singular subject names or refers to one of something—one thing

15

or one person. A plural subject refers to more than one. A subject like *that book* or *the girl* is singular. A subject like *those books* or *the girls* is plural. Two or more singular subjects joined by *and* make a plural subject:

S (= 2)

| Football and hockey | are my favorite sports.

But if two or more singular subjects are joined by *or,* together they make a singular subject. The *or* shows that you are merely referring to one or another of the possibilities.

S (= 1)

| Either light blue or light green | is a good color for the walls.

It is important to know whether a subject is singular or plural because all verbs (and even some X-words) have different forms to go with each.

It is usually easy to tell whether a subject refers to one or more than one. But if the subject is long, a writer or speaker may get mixed up. For instance, no one would have trouble with this subject and X-word:

S   X

| One bolt | **is** missing.

But if there are both plural words and singular words in the subject, it may be harder to decide whether the whole subject refers to one or more than one. For example:

S   X

| One of the boxes of antique dishes | **is** missing.

The subject in this sentence refers to only *one* box of dishes, so that *one* is the word the X-word (*is*) must match. But the plural words *boxes* and *dishes* may make us forget this.

A subject that begins with *one of* or *each* or *every* is always treated as a singular subject, even though it may seem to refer to a number of people or things. For example:

S

| Each starting player on the team | **has** [not *have*] at least four fouls. ·

Some other common words that are always treated as singular are *everybody, everyone, somebody, someone, anyone, nobody,* and *no one.*

16

PRACTICE 1

If the subject of one of these sentences is singular, write the X-word *is* in the blank to complete the sentence. If the subject is plural, write *are*. (Watch out for words like *everybody*.)

1. One of our planes _____ missing.

2. Everyone in the class _____ invited to the party.

3. Half of the students in the class _____ going to a rock concert instead.

4. Mike and Sandy _____ getting married this summer.

5. Nobody who has guessed so far _____ even close.

6. A bundle of unmarked ten dollar bills _____ in the mail for you.

7. Somebody who is heavy and has big feet _____ living upstairs.

8. Each of the items on this counter _____ 49 cents.

2.2 Pro-Nominals

All subjects are **nominals;** that is, they are *noun*-like units. (Whenever we want to show that a unit is a nominal, we will draw a rectangle around it.) Words that can be used in place of nominals are sometimes called *pro-nouns;* however, we will call them **pro-nominals** in this book, to show that they are used for nominals. (*Pro-* = "for.")

The chief reason for using pro-nominals is to avoid repeating nominals. This sentence, for instance, sounds very long and repetitious:

Since those people on the couch near the window have been waiting for over an hour, those people on the couch near the window are a little annoyed.

We can shorten the second part of the sentence by replacing the long subject with the pro-nominal *they:*

Since **those people on the couch near the window** have been waiting for over an hour, **they** are a little annoyed.

17

There are three pro-nominals that are commonly used in edited English to replace *singular subject nominals: it, he,* and *she. He* is used to refer to a man or boy; *she* is used to refer to a woman or girl; and *it* is used to replace almost any other singular subject nominal. (*One* is sometimes used as a pro-nominal to replace a singular nominal beginning with the word *a* or *an;* for example, *I need a good Spanish dictionary. Do you have one?*) The pro-nominal *they* is the pro-nominal most commonly used to replace *plural subject nominals,* although the pro-nominal *we* is used when a person wants to refer to somebody else and himself; for example, *That is a picture of Juan Valdez. We* (= Juan Valdez and I) *went to school together.* (In most grammar books *I* and *you* are also listed with the pro-nominals, but they do not really *replace* nominals: It is true that a speaker uses *I* to refer to himself, but he does not use *I* in place of his own name.)

PRACTICE 2

In each pair of sentences below, the subject nominals are the same. Draw a rectangle around the subject in the second sentence. Then rewrite the sentence using a pro-nominal to replace the subject. (The first one has been done for you.)

1. The first three hundred customers will get prizes.

   $\boxed{\text{The first three hundred customers}}$ will get free cans of dog food.

   They will get free cans of dog food.

2. Bobby Fischer is a great chess player.

   Bobby Fischer is the chess champion of the world.

   _____

3. The longest Frisbee game in history lasted more than two weeks.

   The longest Frisbee game in history went on for seventeen days.

   _____

4. Chess and Frisbee are not very exciting games to watch.

   Chess and Frisbee are more fun to play than they are to watch.

   _____

5. Queen Elizabeth II is the queen of England.

   Queen Elizabeth II is married to Prince Philip, Duke of Edinburgh.

   _____

TASK A

In each empty rectangle write the pro-nominal that could be used in place of the subject nominal just above it. Use *it, he,* or *she* for singular nominals, and *they* for plural nominals. (The first has been done for you.)

1. Karen has been studying music for five years.

   She has been studying rock music for only two years.

2. Rock music was influenced by blues rhythms.

   [ ] was also influenced by jazz.

3. The Rolling Stones are accomplished musicians.

   [ ] are also accomplished performers.

4. Michael P. Jagger is the Stones' leader.

   [ ] is the Stones' main performer.

5. Keith Richards and Mick Jagger do most of the writing for the group.

   [ ] do most of the arranging as well.

6. The concert tour has been a primary activity for the Rolling Stones.

   [ ] has been the one activity most responsible for the group's popularity over the past ten years.

7. Most rock groups can rely on concert touring to keep in touch with their following.

   [ ] can rely on concert touring to make money too.

TASK B

Each sentence about music in this task has a pro-nominal subject. Rewrite the sentences, using full nominals which the pro-nominals could replace.

Example: They are talented rock musicians.

   The Rolling Stones are talented rock musicians.

1. It was popular in the 1950's.

   _____ was popular in the 1950's.

19

2. [It] has its origins in the South, particularly in New Orleans.

_____ has its origins in the South, particularly in New Orleans.

3. [They] must spend many hours on the road.

_____ must spend many hours on the road.

4. [We] spend much of our time listening to records.

_____ spend much of our time listening to records.

5. [She] doesn't like rock as much as I do.

_____ doesn't like rock as much as I do.

6. [They] usually prefer classical guitar.

_____ usually prefer classical guitar.

7. [It] is my favorite kind of music.

_____ is my favorite kind of music.

8. [He] has a singing style that is appealing.

_____ has a singing style that is appealing.

TASK C

Go through the following paragraphs, substituting pro-nominals for nominals that are unnecessarily repeated.

Jazz has often been called the only art form to originate in the United States. Jazz was first played near the end of the nineteenth century. No one really knows where jazz was born, although New Orleans is sometimes called the "cradle of jazz."

Jazz can be thought of as a form of dialogue among musicians. Thus jazz made an abrupt break with the repetitive rhythms of the waltz. The waltz is so precise and mechanical that the waltz seems to call for military dress. On the other hand, a jazz performance is alive; a jazz performance is both creation and composition. At each jazz performance, each musician is part of a conversation, and each musician participates fully in the conversation.

At first, jazz was a simple form of folk music, developed by people who had little or no formal training in music. Today many jazz musicians also know classical music. Many jazz musicians have written and performed music for symphony orchestras.

TASK D

Write three or four sentences describing the style of music of your favorite singer or rock group. Don't repeat nominals unnecessarily.

Agreement

3.1   Ties Between Subjects and X-words

Most of the X-words listed inside the back cover of this book can be used with both singular and plural subjects. For example:

      S   X

My father **can** send me money at any time.

                S   X

The people at the Ford Foundation   **can** send me money at any time.

Can works just as well with the plural subject of the second sentence as it does with the singular subject of the first.

As you have already seen, some X-words, like *am* and *is* and *are,* are used in edited English only with certain subjects. For example:

  S X

I **am** waiting for Dr. Day.

  S X

He **is** very late.

                    S   X

Those people sitting on the couch **aren't** going to wait much longer.

We say that such X-words *agree with* or *tie with* their subjects. (Such **ties** can be shown by means of two-headed arrows, as in the examples that follow.) You can see for yourself that these subjects dictate, or *govern,* the X-words following them: When the subject is changed, the X-word changes, too.

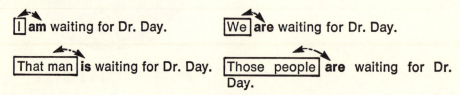

I **am** waiting for Dr. Day.   We **are** waiting for Dr. Day.

That man **is** waiting for Dr. Day.   Those people **are** waiting for Dr. Day.

The X-word *am* is unusual because (in edited English) it is used only with the subject *I*, as in the first example above. (When we are referring to some time in the past, we change the *am* to *was: I am here today; I was here yesterday too.*) The X-words ending in *-s* (those that are italicized in the list) are used only with *singular* subjects—that is, with the subjects *it, he,* and *she,* or with subjects that can be replaced by *it, he,* or *she.* In edited English, no X-word ending in *-s* can be used with a plural subject. With a plural subject, we use *have* instead of *has, do* instead of *does, are* instead of *is,* and *were* instead of *was.* For example:

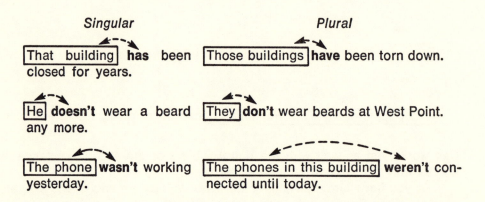

                Singular   *Plural*

That building **has** been closed for years.   Those buildings **have** been torn down.

He **doesn't** wear a beard any more.   They **don't** wear beards at West Point.

The phone **wasn't** working yesterday.   The phones in this building **weren't** connected until today.

Note, however, that in edited English the subject *you* is never followed by an X-word ending in *-s,* even though it may refer to only one person. For example:

Are you sure your name is really George Washington?

Were you the only tap dancer at the rehearsal?

PRACTICE 1

Use the appropriate form of the X-word in parentheses in the blank in each of these sentences.

1. (*have* or *has*)   The names of the Boodle twins _____ not become household words.

2. (*is* or *are*)   Chuck Boodle and his brother Mischa _____ students of knock-knock jokes.

3. (*have* or *has*)   Their attempts to revive this kind of joke

_____ met with little success so far.

4. (*doesn't* or *don't*)   However, failure _____ discourage them.

5. (*does* or *do*)   When Chuck and Mischa's moment _____ come, they will be ready.

6. (*has* or *have*)   Their collection of jokes _____ grown to more than 5,000 knock-knocks.

3.2   Ties Between Subjects and Verbs

Every English verb has two forms for talking about things that happen "now" or "nowadays." One is the **S form** which is used with singular subjects—that is, with the subjects *it, he,* and *she,* or with subjects that can be replaced by *it, he,* or *she.* Here are some examples in which the ties between the subject and the verb are marked:

Captain Riggs lives on a houseboat.

He pays no real estate taxes.

Every month he sails from one port to another.

His wife wishes they lived on land.

She wants to plant a garden, like her sister in Pennsylvania.

Her sister plants different vegetables every spring.

The other form is the **No-S form.** It ties with all subjects that do not require the S form.

But the Riggs children love the houseboat.

They like the sea, and they enjoy moving from port to port.

They want to buy a barge so that their mother can have a floating garden.

Their friends envy their unusual way of life.

You can see the difference between the two forms clearly in this table:

S Forms		No-S Forms	
a person	lives	people	live
the loser	pays	losers	pay
a child	wants	children	want
a student	likes	students	like
he	loves	they	love

The No-S form looks the same as the **base form** of the verb. The base form is the one you would look up in a dictionary if you wanted to know the meaning of the verb. The S form adds an *-s* to the base form to signal a tie with an *it-he-she* subject. In a few verbs, mostly verbs ending in *-s, -sh,* or *-ch,* the S form adds *-es.* For example:

Mrs. Riggs	wishes	Mr. and Mrs. Riggs	wish
she	kisses	they	kiss
a fisherman	catches	fishermen	catch

And also the verb *go:*

a musician	**goes**	musicians	go

Like the X-words *has, does, is,* and *was,* S forms tie with singular subjects. Like the X-words *have, do, are,* and *were,* No-S forms tie with plural subjects.

Sentences that talk about things that are true "now" or about things that happen regularly (or more than once) "nowadays" commonly use either S forms or No-S forms. The S forms—even the S forms of X-words

—always tie with *singular* subjects (that is, with *it-he-she* subjects). For example:

Mrs. Riggs **wants** a garden.

She **doesn't** like living on a houseboat.

PRACTICE 2

Write the appropriate form of the verb in parentheses in the blank in each of these sentences.

1. (*live* or *lives*)   Most people _____ in houses or apartments.

2. (*find* or *finds*)   But some _____ other kinds of places to live in.

3. (*keep* or *keeps*)   For instance, Captain and Mrs. Riggs and their children _____ house on a boat.

4. (*move* or *moves*)   They often _____ from one port to another.

5. (*like* or *likes*)   Captain Riggs _____ the sea.

6. (*want* or *wants*)   Mrs. Riggs _____ to have a garden, but otherwise she is very pleased with the houseboat.

7. (*build* or *builds*)   Bill Hayden, a young man who used to live in New York City, _____ a new tepee every spring.

8. (*live* or *lives*)   He and his wife then _____ in the tepee from June to October.

9. (*take* or *takes*)   For the rest of the year, they _____ care of the houses of people who are traveling.

10. (*live* or *lives*)   In Crete, where the climate is quite mild, some young Americans find caves they can _____ in.

TASK A

Rewrite these ten sentences, following the instructions that appear in parentheses after each one of them. Some changes will require other changes to keep the proper ties between the subjects and verbs. (The first sentence has been done for you.)

1. Even at an early age, a child likes to watch moving things. (Change *a child* to *children*.)

   Even at an early age, children like to watch moving things.

2. Illusions of motion fascinate people of all ages. (Change *illusions of motion* to *the illusion of motion*.)

   _____

   _____

3. We search for new ways to create this illusion. (Change the subject *we* to *a photographer*.)

   _____

   _____

4. Movie cameras are a good example. (Change the subject to *the movie camera*.)

   _____

   _____

5. The movie camera can photograph a series of still pictures in rapid succession. (Omit the X-word *can*.)

   _____

   _____

6. Projectors flash these pictures onto a screen at the same speed. (Change *projectors* to *a projector*.)

   _____

   _____

7. This creates the illusion of motion. (Change to a yes-no question.)

   _____

   _____

TASK B

Each of the following sentences contains the X-word *do* or *does*. Rewrite each sentence omitting the X-word. Change the verbs to S forms when you need to.

1. The camera, the lens, and the lighting *do make* up the tools of the movie photographer.

   _____

   _____

2. The camera lens *does work* very much like the human eye.

   _____

   _____

3. Some lenses *do distort* the image.

   _____

   _____

4. The wide-angle lens *does cause* horizontal and vertical planes to bend.

   _____

   _____

5. The long lens *does produce* much shallower depth relationships.

   _____

   _____

6. Spotlights and floodlights *do provide* all the illumination necessary in film-making.

   _____

   _____

7. A very small quartz bulb *does emit* 500, 750, 1000, and more watts of light.

   _____

   _____

TASK C

Read through the following paragraph once. Then go back over the paragraph and draw a rectangle around the subject in each sentence. Then draw two-headed arrows to show the ties between the subjects and their verbs (or between the subjects and X-words). (The first sentence has been done for you.)

[Television] is not the best way to see movies. Movies on television are cheaper and more convenient than movies shown in theaters. But the viewer misses a lot. For instance, the television screen is too small to do justice to the epic effects in many films. And sometimes the film-maker wants you to see details that get lost on the small screen. Everybody knows how annoying it is when commercials break into the action. A movie shown in a theater continues from beginning to end without interruptions. But most importantly, the viewer at home does not have the same sense of being part of an audience that he gets in the theater. People in a theater do not know each other. Still, they share each other's emotions in a satisfying way.

TASK D

Write a paragraph of seven or eight sentences about some kind of entertainment that interests you. For instance, you could tell what you like or don't like about watching your favorite sport on television, or you could describe how the news is presented on television as compared with its treatment in newspapers. Use verbs that show that the things you are talking about happen "nowadays"—that is, use S forms and No-S forms. When you have finished, go back and mark the subjects and show the ties between the subjects and their verbs, just as you did in Task C.

Writing About Past Time

4.1 X-Words That Signal Past Time

Some X-words, and all verbs that are used without X-words, regularly tie with *it-he-she* subjects. This tie or agreement is shown by the ending *-s* (or *-es*) added to the X-word or verb. Every example you have looked at so far in which this tie appears refers to something that is true *now*, to something that happens regularly or more than once *nowadays*. Here are a few examples from Unit Three:

Captain Riggs lives on a houseboat.

His wife wishes they lived on land.

She wants to plant a garden, like her sister in Pennsylvania.

Her sister plants different vegetables every spring.

It would be possible to add *now* or *nowadays* to most of these sentences:

Captain Riggs lives on a houseboat **now.**

Mrs. Riggs' sister plants different vegetables every spring **nowadays.**

But this is usually not necessary since the tie itself signals "now" or "now-adays." When an X-word or verb has an ending that signals "now" or "now-adays" as in these examples, it is said to be *in the present tense.*

But, of course, we often want to talk about things that happened at some time in the past. Then we usually have to do two things: We have to specify the time we are talking about with a word like *yesterday* or a phrase like *last Saturday,* and we have to use an X-word or verb form that signals past time. X-words and verb forms that show past time are said to be in the *past tense.*

The X-words *is, are,* and *am* cannot be used in sentences about "yes-terday" or "last Sunday." To signal past time, we use the X-word *was* or *were* instead. Notice the difference between the following present and past tense sentences:

(Present)   I **am** a student.

(Past)   Last year I **was** a student.

(Present)   George **is** a sword swallower.

(Past)   Last summer George **was** a sword swallower.

(Present)   We **are** ready to start.

(Past)   We **were** ready to start two hours ago.

The X-word *was* is used with the subject *I* and with all *it-he-she* subjects. *Were* is used with all plural subjects and with *you,* singular or plural. Except for the X-word *was,* there are no special past forms that tie with *it-he-she* subjects. In all other cases, the same past form is used with all subjects, both singular and plural.

PRACTICE 1

Rewrite the following sentences, including the time expression at the left of each to specify the time you are referring to. Use either *was* or *were* in each sentence to signal past time. (Be careful to use the form that ties with the subject in its own sentence. The first sentence has been done.)

1. I am on the dean's list.

    (last term) Last term I was on the dean's list.

         or: I was on the dean's list last term.

2. You are the first person to notice.

    (yesterday) _____.

3. Carol is the captain of her basketball team.

(last season) _____

_____ .

4. The troops are too tired to fight.

(yesterday) _____ .

5. All of you are terrific.

(at the opening last night) _____

_____ .

6. It is hard to drive in the fog.

(early this morning) _____

_____ .

4.2   Verbs: ING Forms and Base Forms

Every English verb has six forms. We have already discussed two of these six forms: the S-form and the No-S form. In addition, every English verb has a form ending in *-ing;* we will call this form the **ING form.**

The ING form of a verb is the form that is used after the X-words *is, are, am, was,* and *were.* We can show this by means of a kind of key like the following:

is
are
am
was
were

↓

living
sitting
standing
writing
lying[1]

---

[1] Note the spelling of *lying:* the *-ie* in *lie* changes to *-y* before the *-ing* ending.

The X-words *is, are,* and *am* are commonly used with ING forms to refer to something that is going on or that is happening *at this moment, right now.* For example:

X   V

Mac and Ina **are sitting** at their desks this very moment.
[Note that the X-word ties with the ING form of the verb.]

Their teacher **is standing** at the blackboard.

He **is writing** on the board.

As you have seen, every verb has an ING form. The ING form is made by adding the ending *-ing* to the base form of the verb: *standing = stand + -ing.* We will call the form *stand* to which the ending *-ing* is added the **base form** of the verb. The base form looks just like the No-S form. The chief difference between them is that the No-S form is regularly used *alone,* to signal present time, while the base form, like the ING form, is usually used after an X-word. The base form is the form that is used after the X-words *can, could, must, should, do,* and *does.* We can show this by adding these other X-words and the base forms to our Verb Key:

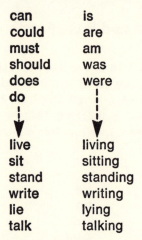

can	is
could	are
must	am
should	was
does	were
do	
live	living
sit	sitting
stand	standing
write	writing
lie	lying
talk	talking

Note how each X-word in this paragraph ties with the form of the verb that follows it:

Mac and Ina are sitting at their desks. Their teacher is writing on

the blackboard. He does not write very clearly. Mac and Ina are talk-

ing to each other. Can't their teacher stop them?

PRACTICE 2

Rewrite each of the following sentences using the correct form (either the base form or the ING form) of the verb indicated between parentheses. Be sure that the verb form you choose ties with the X-word in the sentence. (The first one has been done for you.)

1. (work)   Karen and her friends are <u>working</u> on a jigsaw puzzle.

2. (try)   They are _____ to finish the puzzle.

3. (find)   But they can't _____ the last few pieces.

4. (know)   They don't _____ where they are.

5. (look)   Karen is _____ in the closet that the puzzle was kept in.

6. (know)   She doesn't _____ if she took out all the pieces.

7. (lie)   Look! Several pieces are _____ there on the floor.

8. (take)   Karen should _____ better care of the puzzles.

4.3   Verbs: Past Forms

You have already seen that we regularly use the X-words *is, are,* and *am* —and the X-words *does* and *do*—to signal present time. You have also learned that, to signal past time, we use the X-words *was* and *were,* instead of *is, are,* and *am.*

There is another X-word that we use to signal past time. We use it instead of *do* and *does.* That is the X-word *did.* Note that *did* always ties with some definite time in the past—either a past time that has been expressed in an earlier sentence, or a past time that both the speaker and the hearer know about.

"Where do the Greenbergs live?"

"They live in Manhattan."

"**Did** they live here *last year?*"

"No, they **did**n't. They moved here from Chicago *six months ago.*"

"**Did** you know them then?"

(Like *does* and *do, did* is used with the base form of a verb; for example, *did live, did know, did get*.)

In addition to its base form, its ING form, its S form, and its No-S form, every English verb also has a past form. For most verbs, the past form is made by adding *-d* or *-ed* to the base form. Such verbs are called **regular verbs.** For example:

Base Form			Past Form
live	+ -d	=	lived
talk	+ -ed	=	talked
move	+ -d	=	moved

Sometimes adding *-ed* causes a spelling change:

stop	+ -ed	=	stopped

It may help you to think of past forms as being made up of *did* and the base form; that is, to think that

lived =did live

It is almost as if the *-d* on the end of *lived* jumped from the verb to the *did*, just like the *-s* on the end of *lives:*

lived= did live

For some verbs, called **irregular verbs,** the past form is made by making a sound change as well as a spelling change. For example:

Base Form	Past Form
write	wrote
come	came
go	went
drink	drank
eat	ate
sit	sat
stand	stood

You will find a list of some common irregular verbs on pages 164–65. There is no general rule that will help you much. You simply have to learn the past forms of irregular verbs by heart.

To change a statement with a past form in it into a yes-no question, we move the X-word *did* to the $\tilde{X}$ position; this will leave the base form in the V (=verb) position. For example:

$$\tilde{X} \qquad S \qquad X \quad V$$

The Greenbergs   lived in Chicago last year.

Did the Greenbergs   live   in Chicago last year?

Yes,   they   did live   in Chicago then.

$$\tilde{X} \quad S \quad X \quad V$$

They   came to New York just recently.

Did   they   come to New York just recently?

Note also: They didn't come to New York until six months ago.

Unlike present forms, which have special forms to tie with *it-he-she* subjects, the past forms of verbs are the same, whatever the subject: *I moved, he moved, they moved,* etc.

PRACTICE 3

Write the appropriate past form of the verbs in parentheses in the blanks below. If you are not sure of one of the irregular verbs, you can look up its past form on pages 164–65. (The first one has been done for you.)

1. (sleep)   I __slept__ very well last night.

2. (eat)   I _____ a large stack of pancakes for breakfast.

3. (love)   Romeo _____ Juliet.

4. (drive)   We _____ slowly this morning because of the fog.

5. (go)   Suddenly something _____ wrong with the radiator.

6. (give)   Mike _____ his girl a partridge in a pear tree.

7. (think)   The base runner _____ he was safe.

8. (lose)   I _____ my car keys yesterday afternoon.

9. (find)   I _____ them this morning.

10. (like)   At first, he _____ Joan better than Mary.

4.4 Ties with Past Time

Always remember that there are two things we must do when we write about the past: We must use the appropriate forms of the X-words or verbs, and we must mention the specific time in the past that we are thinking of. But we do not have to keep on repeating the past time to which we are referring. We simply mention *last Sunday,* for instance, in the first sentence we write about whatever it was that happened then. After that, we don't have to mention the time again until we change and start talking about some other time. As long as we are speaking of the events of last Sunday, we keep on using past forms. And all of these past forms tie with *last Sunday,* the specific past time that we have already mentioned. For example:

I had tickets to the ballet *last Sunday,* but I had a bad cold and couldn't

go. So I gave them to Wendy and her boy friend.

When a new time in the past is mentioned, the verbs and X-words that relate to that time tie with it.

Last month Charlie told me he was broke and couldn't pay me back.

I saw him *yesterday,* and it was the same story.

It sometimes happens that we are talking about a time or event in the past that does not have to be specified, since our reader knows the specific time (or at least the general time) to which we are referring. In such a situation, of course, we do not have to use a time-expression. Here is an example:

Napoleon died on the island of St. Helena.

PRACTICE 4

Show the ties between the X-words or verbs in the following sentences, and the specific times to which they relate. Use dotted arrows with two heads, like those in the examples above.

1. The Chipmunks won their first game of the season last night. The

other team didn't show up, so they won by default.

2. The year before last I took some guitar lessons. Then last year I took up the snare drum.

3. I studied all last night for my math test. This morning I found out that there wasn't one.

4. On the first day Grace didn't care much for her new job. By the second day she hated it.

5. Marvin was very lucky last Thursday. He won the lottery, but that wasn't all. His girl agreed to marry him.

TASK A

The following is a transcript of notes made by a private detective shadowing a suspect. The detective recorded his notes on a miniature tape recorder in his pocket. He intended to type them up later on. In doing so, he intended to change all of the present forms to past forms, leaving the rest of his sentences pretty much as he had recorded them. But you are asked to help him out by making the changes for him. Go through his notes, changing all present X-words and verb forms to their past forms. You can write the past forms directly above the present forms. (The first sentence has been done for you.)

At 9:33 A.M. Friday the suspect ~~leaves~~ **left** his apartment building accompanied by a large German shepherd. He starts toward Fifty-ninth Street. There are two hydrants on the block, and the dog stops at both. The suspect seems impatient and pulls at the leash. At the corner of Fifty-ninth, the suspect looks around furtively. I think we are onto something at last.

Suddenly, the suspect hails a cab which is heading south. He speaks to the driver of the cab. He puts the dog in the cab and watches the cab drive off. The cab turns in the direction of Central Park.

I follow the suspect at a discreet distance to a bar on Lexington Avenue. He orders a Bloody Mary. To avoid suspicion, I order a beer. The bartender seems to know the suspect. He asks him if he is taking the dog for a walk in the park again. The suspect says the brute loves his exercise. He orders another drink.

Half an hour later, I trail the suspect back to the corner of Park and Fifty-ninth. The cab is already there with the meter running. I can't see what he pays the driver, but it looks like ten dollars.

The suspect returns to the apartment with the dog. I go back to my post at the bus stop.

TASK B

Each of the verbs below is an irregular verb. (That is, its past form is not made by adding -d or -ed.) Use the list on pages 164–65 to find the past forms. Then write one sentence for each verb, in which you describe something that happened *yesterday*. Follow the example below.

Example:

    break   My sister broke her leg skiing yesterday.

1. become   _____

2. keep   _____

3. begin   _____

4. bring   _____

5. choose   _____

6. know   _____

TASK C

Rewrite the following passage, changing all the underlined present X-words and verb forms to past forms and all the underlined past X-words and verb forms to present forms.

"Now! Now!" <u>cries</u> the Queen. "Faster! Faster!" And they <u>go</u> so fast that at last they <u>seem</u> to skim through the air, hardly touching the ground with their feet, till suddenly, just as Alice <u>is</u> getting quite exhausted, they <u>stop,</u> and she <u>finds</u> herself sitting on the ground, breathless and giddy.

The Queen <u>props</u> her up against a tree, and <u>says</u> kindly, "You may rest a little, now."

Alice <u>looks</u> round her in great surprise. "Why, I <u>did</u> believe we've been under this tree the whole time! Everything's just as it was!"

"Of course it <u>was,</u>" <u>says</u> the Queen. "What would you have it?"

"Well, in our country," <u>says</u> Alice, still panting a little, "you'd generally get to somewhere else—if you ran very fast for a long time as we <u>had</u> been doing."

"A slow sort of country!" <u>says</u> the Queen. "Now, here, you <u>saw</u> it <u>took</u> all the running you <u>could</u> do, to keep in the same place. If you <u>wanted</u> to get somewhere else, you must run at least twice as fast as that!"

—from *Through the Looking Glass*
by Lewis Carroll.

TASK D

Write five or six sentences that describe an action as though you were doing it right now. (You might imagine that you are talking into a pocket tape recorder, like the private eye in Task A.) You might describe getting to school, meeting someone for a date, or going home for a holiday. Or, if you want, you can be a private eye shadowing someone. Use the present forms of X-words and verbs throughout. Then go back over your sentences, writing in past forms above the present forms, just as you did in Task A.

Sentence Trunks

5.1   Subjects and Predicates

The essential part of a sentence is called the **trunk,** just like the main part of a body or the main part of a tree. The trunk of a sentence is made up of two important parts, the **subject** and the **predicate.** You already know what the subject is and how to find it. (If you are hazy about subjects, you may want to look back at Section 1.1 in Unit 1.) The predicate is everything in the trunk except the subject—that is, everything that is not part of the subject.

Some simple sentences are all trunk; they have nothing in them either before or after the trunk. We will mark the subject with an *S,* and draw a box around it, as we did earlier. We will mark the predicate *P* and draw a wavy arrow above it pointing to the subject, to show that it usually says something about the subject.

$$P$$

$$S \longleftarrow\!\!\sim\!\!\sim\!\!\sim\!\!\sim\!\!\sim\!\!\sim$$

Ann married Bill.

But many sentences contain something more, in addition to the trunk: They also contain one or more other units, which give additional information of some sort. These additional units say something *about* the trunk; and they can come either after or before the trunk. For instance, to that

43

last example about Ann's marrying Bill, we can add another unit, giving the reason why Ann married Bill:

T

Ann married Bill (because she wanted to settle down.

or:

T

Because she wanted to settle down,) Ann married Bill.

Note that this additional unit can be placed either after or before the trunk (which is marked *T*). The wavy arrow under *because she wanted to settle down* shows that it says something more about the trunk. (We will be looking at more additions like this one in Unit Six, after we have taken a look at the predicate part of trunks. For now, just remember that we will be using a large parenthesis mark to separate the trunk from the units that are added to it. Notice that the parenthesis always curves away from the trunk.)

PRACTICE 1

The following ten sentences consist of trunks with nothing else added. Draw a box around the subject in each, and label it *S*. Then draw a wavy arrow over the predicate, pointing toward the subject. Label the predicate *P*. (The first one has been done for you.)

P

S

1. Money isn't everything.

2. Sergeant Malloy used to work in the recruiting office.

3. The sergeant liked to describe the advantages of joining the Army.

4. He spoke glowingly of travel to interesting places.

5. Vocational training was also a major theme in his talks to recruits.

6. The young men were always impressed.

7. The sergeant forgot himself.

8. He would start shouting commands and telling the men to shape up.

9. This discouraged potential recruits.

10. Sergeant Malloy has been reassigned.

5.2   The Positions in a Predicate

The wavy arrow that we draw over the predicate pointing toward the subject shows that the predicate says something about the subject.

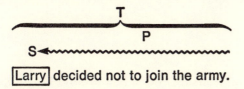

Larry decided not to join the army.

The predicate has three positions in it: the X position (which you know about already), for X-words; the M position (for "middle"), for *not, n't,* and words like *never, often,* and *already;* and the Y position for the rest of the predicate. For example:

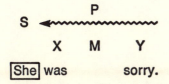

Either the X position or the M position—or both—may be unfilled:

S ←〜〜〜〜〜〜〜〜〜〜〜P

X   M   Y

She was   sorry.

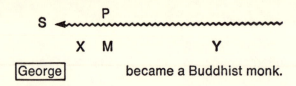

George   became a Buddhist monk.

Occasionally, the word that fills the M position shifts around the X-word and turns up in what we will call the shifted M position (that is, the M̃ position).

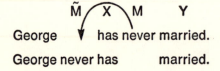

George   ▼ has never married.

George never has   married.

We will be looking at the Y position, and at the units that fill it, in Section 5.3.

PRACTICE 2

The following sentences are all trunks. Draw a box around the subject in each and then mark the three positions in each predicate. (As for the Y position, which we have not really discussed yet, just remember that it includes everything that does not fill the X and M—or M̃—positions.)

If an X or M position is not filled, insert a caret in the proper place, and then write the symbol above the line. (The first one has been done for you.)

           X M   Y

1. ⎡Sergeant Malloy⎤ was ∧ a career man.

2. Mr. Davis has already filed his tax forms.

3. He must be expecting a refund.

4. Malloy was not a very good recruiter.

5. Ann often thinks of George.

6. Her parents have never regretted the fact that she married Bill.

5.3 Predicators

Another way of saying that a predicate says something about the subject is to say that it "makes a predication about the subject." The part of the predicate that really makes the predication is the part we have been marking Y. We will call this part the **predicator,** and we will label it *Pr.*

There are several different kinds of units that can go in the Y position to make a predication. We will look at them one at a time.

The predicator may be a **nominal**—that is, a noun-like unit.

```
    S     X      Y
  Mr. Dix is a good teacher .               (Pr = nominal)
```

The predicator may be an **adjective** or an **adjectival.** An adjective is a word like *beautiful, tall,* or *happy* that can be used after the word *very* or between the word *the* and a noun, as in *very happy* or *the tall building.* The predicator in this next example is an adjective:

```
  S X   M      Y
  He is always pleasant.                    (Pr = adjective)
```

An adjectival is an adjective-like unit. The words *very sick* make up an adjectival in this example:

```
    S        X      Y
  The patient was very sick.                (Pr = adjectival)
```

The predicator may be a **prepositional phrase.** A prepositional phrase is a unit that begins with a **preposition** (that is, a word like *in, on, at, from, of, up, behind,* or even several words like *in front of* and *because of*) and that ends with a nominal or pro-nominal. The predicators in the following examples are prepositional phrases:

```
    S     X    Y
  Mr. Dix is at his desk.                   (Pr = prepositional phrase)
```

```
        S         X   M     Y
  My little brother is always in trouble.
```

```
      S      X      Y
  The garage is in back of the house.
```

Notice that the nominal and adjectival predicators state what the subject *is* or *was*:

> Her father is **a tailor.**
>
> The load was **very heavy.**

Prepositional phrases also give information about the subject when they are used as predicators:

> He is **at his desk.**
>
> Mrs. Smith was **in the hospital** for three weeks.

We will call predicators like these **complements.** A complement can always be placed directly after *is, are, was,* or *were* following a subject nominal, as in the examples above.

PRACTICE 3

The underlined part of each of the following sentences is a predicator. Decide whether the predicator is a nominal, an adjective, or a prepositional phrase. Then fill in the name of the proper unit after the "equals" sign. (The first one has been done for you.)

1. Sergeant Malloy was the U.S. chief recruiting officer   (Pr = nominal)

2. The doctor is in his office.   (Pr =)

3. This milk is sour.   (Pr =)

4. Our Persian cat is up that tree.   (Pr =)

5. The tree is in front of the house.   (Pr =)

6. The last problem was tricky.   (Pr =)

7. George is a Buddhist monk.   (Pr =)

5.4 Predicatids

Another kind of predicator that can fill the Y position in the predicate is called a **predicatid.** Here are some examples:

S   X   Y

Mr. Dix is **correcting his students' papers.**   (Pr = predicatid)

S   X M Y

That radio doesn't **work.**   (Pr = predicatid)

These predicators are *not* complements. They do not state what the subject *is*. Rather, they state what the subject is doing, does, or doesn't do.

A predicatid may consist of only one word or of more than one. But it always contains a time-less verb form; that is, a verb form that does not signal either present time or past time. The ING form in the first example above is a time-less form of this kind, as is the base form in the second example. In addition to the verb form, which must be present, a predicatid may also include an **object.** Like subjects, objects are always nominals (or pro-nominals). For example:

Y

S   X M   V   O

Mr. Dix is still correcting **his students' papers.**

Y

S X M V O

Ann did not marry George.

She did not marry him.

Notice that an object refers to something or someone other than the subject. In this way it is different from a complement, which tells what the subject is.

Some verbs do not take objects. After such verbs, the object position remains unfilled:

Y

S   X   M   V   O

George has never married

The last kind of predicator that can fill the Y position in the predicate is a **time-oriented predicator**—that is, a predicator beginning with either a past verb form or a present verb form. For example:

```
              Y
           ⏜⏜⏜
  S   X   M   V   O
[Ann]      married Bill.
```

Since time-oriented predicators always begin with past or present verb forms, they cannot occur together with X-words. In other words, the X position before such predicators will always be unfilled.

PRACTICE 4

The time-oriented predicators in the following sentences are underlined. Label the verb in each *V*. If there is an object, label it *O*. (The first one has been done for you.)

```
            V      O
```
1. Mr. Tanaka took a picture.

2. The detective overlooked an important clue.

3. As a result, the criminal escaped.

4. Mrs. Morrison owns an oil well.

5. Our team loses every game.

6. The players always fumble the ball.

7. Angie takes tap-dancing lessons.

8. She wants a career in musical comedy.

TASK A

Draw a box around the subject in each of the following sentences and label it *S*. Then draw a wavy arrow over the predicate, with the point toward the subject. Label the predicate *P*. Then, on the blank line, copy the whole predicate (including the X-word), and mark the X, M, and Y positions. Remember that the X and M positions are not always filled. (The first sentence has been done for you.)

P

S ←〰〰〰〰〰〰〰〰〰〰〰〰〰〰〰〰〰〰

1. (Trunk) ‖Plants and small trees‖ are often used in decorating
〰〰
homes.

X M   Y

(Predicate)   are often used in decorating homes

2. (Trunk)   Different plants can create different moods.

(Predicate)   _____

3. (Trunk)   A small palm tree gives an air of formality.

(Predicate)   _____

4. (Trunk)   An orange tree is a colorful addition to a room.

(Predicate)   _____

5. (Trunk)   Geraniums and other small plants may sometimes give

a feeling of warmth and intimacy.

(Predicate)   _____

6. (Trunk)   Plants will frequently bring life to an otherwise lifeless

room.

(Predicate)   _____

7. (Trunk)   Plants also help to preserve the proper proportion of oxy-

gen and carbon dioxide in the air.

(Predicate)   _____

_____

8. (Trunk)   They can take in carbon dioxide from the air.

(Predicate)   _____

9. (Trunk)   They give off needed oxygen.

(Predicate)   _____

10. (Trunk)   City dwellers should always have plants in their homes.

(Predicate)   _____

TASK B

Write a predicate that will complete each of these unfinished sentences. Use an X-word in each of your predicates and add the kind of
predicator called for in the instructions. (You may refer back to Sections
5.3 and 5.4 if you need to.) You may fill the M position or leave it empty,
depending on your own sentence. (The first sentence has been done for
you. The X, V, and O positions have been marked in the first sentence, but
you do not have to mark the positions in your own sentences.)

1. (Use a V O predicatid as the predicator.) The first defense witness

$$\underbrace{ \overset{Y}{}}$$

X   V   O

was telling his story. _____

2. (Use a prepositional phrase as the predicator.) The dog house

_____

3. (Use a nominal as the predicator.) Her father _____

_____

4. (Use an adjective as the predicator.) House plants _____

_____

5. (Use a V O predicatid as the predicator.) His best friend _____

_____

6. (Use a prepositional phrase as the predicator.) My car _____

_____

7. (Use an adjective as the predicator.) Carol's painting _____

_____

8. (Use a V O predicatid as the predicator.) The politician _____

_____

TASK C

The following paragraph describes an object by telling what it is *not*, rather than what it is. Read it through once; then go back and mark the X positions, and draw boxes around the subjects and wavy arrows over the predicates. Mark the subjects *S* and the predicates *P*. (The first sentence has been done for you.)

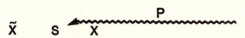

An orange is not like any other fruit. It is not as large as a grapefruit. It is not as small as a lime, either. Its color is not as yellow as that of a lemon, but it is not quite as red as the color of a tomato. The skin of an orange is not as smooth as the skin of an apple, but it is not as rough as the skin of a pineapple. Oranges are not as sweet as plums. They are not as tart as lemons. They do not smell like the other citrus fruits. The orange is not a common fruit.

TASK D

Write a paragraph like the one in Task C in which you describe an object, a person, or a place in terms of what it, he, or she is *not*.

Shifters

6.1 Front and End Shifters

The trunk of a sentence, which contains the subject and the predicate, is the main part of the sentence. But as we saw in Section 5.1, some sentences also contain something more, in addition to the trunk; they contain some other word or word group that can come either before or after the trunk and that "says something about" the trunk. For example:

P

F   S ⬅〰〰〰〰

Last year Ann got married.

P

F   S ⬅〰〰〰〰

Because she wanted to settle down, she married Bill.

The bold-faced words in these sentences fill **the front position** at the front of the sentence, *in front of* the subject. We will mark this position F (for "Front"). Word groups like these that can fill the F position in a sentence can also come *after* the trunk. That is why they are called **shifters:** They can *shift* around the trunk, from the Front position to the End position at the end of the sentence. (We will mark the End position E.) For example:

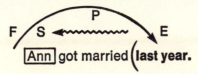

55

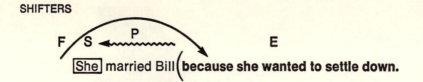

F / S ←〜〜〜〜〜 P

She married Bill (because she wanted to settle down.

From now on we will cut a shifter off from the trunk with a big parenthesis mark, as in these last two examples.

One of the most common uses for shifters is to give information about *time.* For example:

F   S ←〜〜〜〜〜〜〜〜 P

Yesterday) Dr. Day was late to work.

S ←〜〜〜〜〜〜 P   E

Dr. Day was late to work (yesterday.

But shifters are also used to give other kinds of information. For instance, the shifter in the next example gives information about the *place* where something happened:

F   S ←〜〜 P

In the middle of the bridge,) his car stalled.

S ←〜〜〜 P   E

His car stalled (in the middle of the bridge.

And the shifter in the next example gives a *reason* for the predication that is made in the trunk:

F   S ←〜〜〜〜〜

Because of a faulty generator,) the motor went dead.

S ←〜〜〜〜   E

The motor went dead (because of a faulty generator.

Shifters often give information about the *manner* in which something happened:

F   S ←〜〜〜〜

Suddenly) his car stopped.

56

S ◄〜〜〜〜   E

[His car] stopped (suddenly.

or

F   S ◄〜〜〜〜〜〜〜〜〜〜

Without any warning) [his car] came to a complete stop.

S ◄〜〜〜〜〜〜〜〜〜〜〜〜   E

[His car] came to a complete stop (without any warning.

A shifter that fills the F position in a sentence usually has to be shifted to the E position before its sentence can be changed into a yes-no question:

X̃   F   S X ◄〜〜〜〜〜 E

Last year [Ann]   got married.

S

Did   [Ann]   get married (last year?

Yes,   [Ann] did get married (last year.

PRACTICE 1

The following sentences have shifters in the F position. Change the sentences into yes-no questions. To do so, you will first have to move the shifters to the E position. Label the shifter in both the statement and the question. (The first one has been done for you.)

F

1. Last night) her boyfriend didn't call.

E

Her boyfriend didn't call (last night. _____

Didn't her boyfriend call last night? _____

2. Before the game started, Coach Brown was certain of victory.

_____

_____

3. For many days he had studied films of his opponents' games.

_____

_____

4. Even before they called it, he was sure what each play would be.

_____

_____

5. Because of their coach's careful preparation, all of the players were confident.

_____

_____

6.2 Two or More Shifters

There may be more than one shifter in a sentence. Two or even three shifters can fill the F position or the E position (or both at the same time). For example:

     F1   F2

The next day,) on his way home from work,) Mr. Frank bought a puppy

        E

(because he was lonely.

                E1   E2

He walked his dog (every evening (right after dinner.

Each shifter has to be checked separately to see if it can be moved from one position to the other. For example:

      F   T

The next day,) Mr. Frank bought a puppy.

              T   E

    Mr. Frank bought a puppy (the next day.

F

On his way home from work) Mr. Frank bought a puppy.

E

Mr. Frank bought a puppy (on his way home from work.

E

Mr. Frank bought a puppy (because he was lonely.

F

Because he was lonely,) Mr. Frank bought a puppy.

When there are several shifters in the F position, they must all be moved to the E position when a statement is changed into a yes-no question:

F1   F2

Later tonight,) when the rates go down,) Grace will call.

E1   E2

Will Grace call (later tonight (when the rates go down?

PRACTICE 2

In each of the following sentences, there is an empty F or E position, shown by a blank. Fill in each blank with a word or group of words that could be shifted from the F position to the E position or from the E position to the F position without changing the meaning of the sentence. (The first sentence has been done for you.)

1. _____, he began looking for a job.

   Because he was running out of money, he began looking for a job.

2. He looked in the want ads _____.

3. _____, he found nothing suitable.

4. Then, _____, he found the ad he had been waiting for.

5. He thought he would make a good bartender, _____

   _____.

TASK A

Rewrite the following sentences, shifting each front shifter to the end position in its sentence, and each end shifter to the front position. (In some sentences there are no shifters; in others there are two or even more.) Mark each front position with a parenthesis and an *F*. Mark each end position with a parenthesis and an *E*. (If there are no shifters in a sentence, both the F and E positions in that sentence, of course, will remain empty.)
Example:

In today's world,) the effect of advertising is incalculable.

F   E

The effect of advertising is incalcuable(in today's world.

or:

                                  E

Advertising is big business, (no matter how you look at it.

                F   E

No matter how you look at it,) advertising is big business.

or:

Merchants have always tried to advertise their wares.

F   E

Merchants have always tried to advertise their wares.

1. Many years ago, the human voice was the principal advertising medium.

2. Village criers shouted out their advertising messages.

3. Babylonian merchants hired barkers to call attention to the goods they had for sale.

4. In Egyptian ports, the arrival of ships and their cargoes was advertised by criers.

_____

_____

5. Around the year 3000 B.C., the Babylonians began cutting the name of the temple in each of the bricks used in its construction.

_____

_____

_____

6. During the thousand years of the Dark Ages, civilization seemed to go backward.

_____

_____

7. Around A.D. 300, merchants used barkers at fairs in Britain.

_____

8. In many European cities, town criers walked up and down the streets calling out official announcements during the twelfth and thirteenth centuries.

_____

_____

_____

9. Since the art of paper-making did not reach Europe until the twelfth century, the merchants of earlier centuries were not able to pass out "fliers" describing their wares.

_____

_____

_____

10. Scribes wrote advertisements by hand in the fifteenth century.

_____

TASK B

Test each sentence below for front or end shifters. If you find either a front shifter or an end shifter, cut it off from its trunk by means of an outward-facing parenthesis. Mark each shifter *F* or *E* depending upon which position it is in, and mark each trunk *T*. Then bring down the trunk—only the trunk—onto the blank line provided beneath each sentence, and mark the two X positions (supplying *do, does,* or *did* if necessary). Draw a box around the subject and mark it *S;* and finally, mark the predicate *P,* and draw a wavy arrow over it pointing to the subject.
Example:

F   **T**

In Pompeii) announcements for real estate were printed on street walls.

  X̃   **S**   **X**   **P**

             | announcements for real estate | were printed on street walls

1. Around 1480, the first printed advertisement appeared.

_____

2. William Caxton was the first English printer, as you probably know.

_____

3. Although signboards continued to be popular, printing gave advertising a tremendous boost.

_____

4. Very quickly, merchants began to make use of printed "fliers."

_____

5. A few years later, leading English artists and engravers were illustrating handbills and posters.

_____

6. In olden times, laws were "proclaimed" publicly by town criers.

_____

7. By the 1700's, printed handbills and posters commonly informed the public about new laws.

_____

8. By the eighteenth century, English newspapers were thriving on advertising.

---

9. In America, the first advertising appeared on the signboards of taverns.

---

10. In spite of the British ban on newspapers, Benjamin Franklin printed a newspaper called the *Pennsylvania Gazette.*

TASK C

Cut off front and end shifters in the following passage with large parentheses. Label each shifter *F* or *E* according to its position. (In many sentences, of course, there will be no shifters.)

By the middle of the 1700's, newspapers had grown in size and variety. Previously all advertisements had been placed at the back of the newspaper. Now some appeared toward the front. In 1784, the first newspaper to become a daily became one largely because it had so much advertising.

Advertising increased after the Civil War. Goods were no longer made in one's or two's at home. Instead they were being produced in large quantities at factories. It was cheaper to make them this way, but advertising was needed to help sell all that was produced.

The first American magazines appeared in the mid-1880's. They were literary publications with many essays and poems but not many readers. Their publishers resisted advertising in their pages until the need for additional money became great. Over a period of several years, one publisher after another gave in and began to run ads. A man named J. Walter Thompson had a great deal to do with convincing publishers to accept advertising. The advertising agency that bears his name is the largest in the world today.

. . . Radio advertising started in 1922. By 1928, there were five hundred stations. At first, radio advertising consisted of little more than an announcement of the name of the company and its product. We must assume that such advertising must have produced sales because advertising budgets were large even then. One automobile manufacturer spent half a million dollars on radio in 1928. In the 1930's, radio advertisements (which are called commercials) became longer and included comments on the benefits of the product or service advertised. In some cases, playlets even dramatized the use of the product or service.

—Adapted from *Advertising* (A First Book)
by Richard O. Pompian.

TASK D

Write five or six sentences about some topic that interests you, using front and end shifters in each of them. The topic may be a sport that you are interested in, a fad or fashion, or anything else you want to write about. Use your shifters to give (additional) information about *place,* about *time,* or about the *reasons* things happened as they did, or even about the *manner* in which things happened—that is, the way they happened.

Compounds

7.1 Compound Subjects

One of the features of mature writing is the large number of "packed" sentences—that is, sentences packed with more than just one or two pieces of new information. A young child just learning to write commonly states his ideas in a string of short, choppy sentences, but a mature writer is much more likely to pull his ideas together into longer and more informative sentences. In the next few units we will be looking at some of the different devices for **combining** ideas in sentences. We will begin with the most common device—**compounding.**

Frequently, the same parts of two or more sentences can be combined into one with the help of a **coordinator.** That is, two or more subjects, or trunks, or predicates, can be joined together into single units by means of coordinators. The coordinators that join these similar parts are words like *and, but, or,* and *so.* A single unit that is made up by joining two units together with a coordinator is said to be a **compound.**

For example, look at these two sentences:

S

The captain deserted the ship.

S

The crew deserted the ship too.

Instead of using two sentences, we can convey the same information in a single sentence by compounding the subject.

S

```
        +
┌────────────────────────┐
│ The captain and the crew│ deserted the ship.
└────────────────────────┘
```

(The coordinator is marked by means of a little "+" sign written above it.)
   A coordinator may be used to combine more than two items. For instance, the subject of this next sentence can be joined with the two subjects we have already compounded:

S

```
┌────────────┐
│ The officers│ deserted the ship as well.
└────────────┘
```

Then our sentence would have a subject made up of three parts:

S

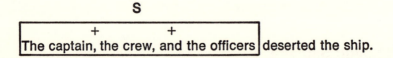

```
        +            +
┌────────────────────────────────────────┐
│ The captain, the crew, and the officers │ deserted the ship.
└────────────────────────────────────────┘
```

Note that the *and* between the first two items in a three-part compound is left out and replaced by a comma. In such cases, a second comma is regularly added before the *and* that comes between the second and third items.
   The coordinator *or* is also used in forming compound subjects. For example:

S

```
┌────────┐
│ A poker│ may have been the murder weapon.
└────────┘
```

S

```
┌────────────┐
│ A lead pipe│ may have been the murder weapon.
└────────────┘
```

S

```
           +
┌─────────────────────┐
│ A poker or a lead pipe│ may have been the murder weapon.
└─────────────────────┘
```

You should note, however, that although compound subjects formed by using the coordinator *and* are always plural, those formed by using the coordinator *or* are often singular. Look at the examples at the top of the next page.

66

S

+   +

The captain, the crew, and the officers **are** being tried for abandoning their ship.

S

+

A poker or a lead pipe **is** believed to have been the murder weapon.

PRACTICE 1

Draw a box around the subject in each of the following paired sentences. Then, in the space provided, combine the two subjects into a compound subject, using either the coordinator *and* or *or.* (The first one has been done for you.)

1. A history professor witnessed the theft.

   Six boy scouts witnessed the theft.

   <u>A history professor and six boy scouts witnessed the theft.</u>

2. The White House denied the charges.

   The Pentagon denied the charges.

   _____.

3. Metaphors are figures of speech.

   Similes are figures of speech.

   _____.

4. A friend may write the recommendation.

   A relative may write the recommendation.

   _____.

5. A B average is required for admission.

    The instructor's permission is required for admission.

---

6. Susan is sure to win first prize.

    Penny is sure to win first prize.

7.2 Other Compound Units

Predicates, objects, and even shifters, can be compounded, as well as subjects.

    Compound Predicates. These two sentences can be written as separate sentences:

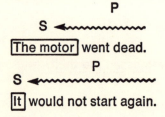

Or, the predicates can be combined into a compound predicate, since *both predicates have the same subject, in the original sentences.* For example:

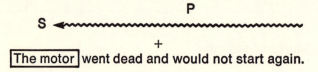

There may even be three or more parts to a compound predicate:

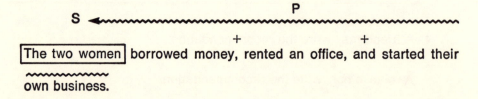

Notice that a series of predicates, like a series of subjects, is punctuated with a comma between each item and a comma in addition to *and* between the last two items. This is the usual punctuation for all compound elements. Four items, for example, would be punctuated like this: A, B, C, and D.

Compound Objects. The object following a verb can also be a compound:

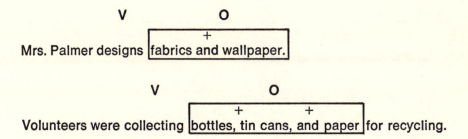

Compound Shifters. Two or more shifters can be joined together to form a compound shifter:

E
+
The motor went dead (because of a faulty generator or because of a loose wire.

F
+
During the evening and on weekends,) telephone rates are lower.

PRACTICE 2

Combine the following numbered groups of sentences into one sentence each, by compounding the predicates, objects, or shifters. (The first one has been done for you.)

1. The campers went on hikes.

   They took canoe trips.

   The campers went on hikes and took canoe trips.

2. Ann plays tennis after work.

   She plays tennis on weekends.

3. At the ball game, the boys ate hot dogs.

They ate popcorn.

They ate peanuts.

_____.

4. The workers voted a strike.

They walked out of the factory.

_____.

5. Mr. Micawber never saved money.

He never lived within his means.

_____.

6. Every evening Marie works as a waitress.

All day Saturday Marie works as a waitress.

_____.

7.3 Compound Sentences and Sentence-Units

The following sentences can be written like this:

Charlie was late to school on Monday.
He was early on Tuesday.

Or they can be combined in this way:

+

Charlie was late to school on Monday, but he was early on Tuesday.

When two (or more) whole sentences are combined into one with the help of a coordinator, the result is what we call a **compound sentence.** We will call the two (or three) parts of a compound sentence—each of which would be a full sentence if it was written separately with a capital letter at the beginning and a period at the end—**sentence-units** or **S-units.**

Every S-unit *must* contain a trunk. It may also include one or more shifters. For example:

         T

                                        +

The captain was discharged for deserting his ship, and

        T

the crew was reprimanded.

        T   **E**

                              +

Eric worked at the post office (all day long, so

       T   **E**

he could only work on his novel (at night.

It is customary to separate two S-units with a comma in addition to a co-ordinator, or else to separate them with a semicolon alone without any coordinator. (When both a comma and a coordinator are used together, the comma comes just before the coordinator.) For example, the sentence about Charlie can be punctuated in either of these two ways:

                            +

Charlie was late to school on Monday, but he was early on Tuesday.

or:

                            +

Charlie was late to school on Monday; he was early on Tuesday.

You should always remember that there is an important difference between a compound sentence and a compound predicate. All the parts of a compound predicate have *the same subject,* which is stated once at the beginning of the whole sentence. Each of the parts of a compound sentence, on the other hand, consists of a complete sentence-unit, each with its own subject and predicate (and possibly, also, with one or more shifters). Compare the *compound predicate* in the first example at the top of the next page with the *compound sentences* in the second and third examples.

P

S ◀〜〜〜〜〜〜〜〜〜〜〜〜〜〜〜〜〜〜〜〜〜〜〜〜〜
+
General Snap loved inspections and had lots of them.

P   P

S ◀〜〜〜〜〜〜〜〜〜〜〜〜   S ◀〜〜〜〜〜〜〜〜〜〜〜〜
+
General Snap loved inspections, but his men thought them a waste
〜〜〜
of time.

P

S ◀〜〜〜〜〜〜〜〜〜〜〜〜   S ◀〜〜〜〜〜〜〜〜〜〜〜〜
+
General Snap loved inspections, but his men thought them a waste

E
〜〜〜
of time (except on very special occasions.

PRACTICE 3

Mark the coordinator in each of the following sentences with a +. Then, in the space provided, state whether the coordinator joins the parts of a compound predicate or the parts of a compound sentence. (The first one has been done for you.)

+
1. General Snap loved inspections, so he had a lot of them.

_____ a compound sentence _____

2. The workers voted a strike and walked out of the factory.

_____

3. Mr. Micawber never saved money or lived on a budget.

_____

4. It takes more than money to be happy, but money helps a lot.

_____

5. Whales are mammals, and they must come to the surface to breathe.

_____

6. The Haydens moved out of their apartment and built a tepee in the woods.

_____

7. Marie goes to school days and works nights.

_____

TASK A

Mark the coordinator in each of the following sentences by placing a + over it. Then, on the line provided to the right of each sentence, state whether the coordinator joins the parts of a compound sentence, the parts of a compound predicate, the parts of a compound subject, the parts of a compound front shifter, or the parts of a compound end shifter. (The first one has been done for you.)

         +
1. Cats and dogs should have their own private spots in the house.

_____a compound subject_____

2. They often want to be left alone and actually do need privacy at times.

_____

3. If an animal cannot find a private spot of his own or if he is prevented from establishing his own territory, he will become bad-tempered.

_____

4. A dog likes to have a regular place to sleep, but a cat needs many different places to hide in.

_____

5. Cats and dogs do not like to be disturbed when they are resting in their own private spots.

_____

6. They are very much like human beings in that way and in many others.

_____

7. People may know this, but all too often they act as if they didn't.

_____

8. Very often, pet owners annoy their pets and frustrate them.

_____

9. Eventually, a pet will turn against such an owner and will avoid him as much as possible.

_____

10. If an animal has enough food and if he is left alone to rest in his own private spot, he will probably be a happy pet.

_____

TASK B

Combine the sentences in each of the following sets according to the bracketed instructions. (The first one has been done for you.)

1. The boat raced past the dock.
   The water-skier fell down.
   [Form a compound sentence, using a comma and a coordinator.]

   The boat raced past the dock, and the water-skier fell down.

   _____

2. The monkeys saw no evil.
   They heard no evil.
   They spoke no evil.
   [Combine the predicates into a compound predicate.]

   _____

   _____

3. In the fall, the days grow shorter.
   In the spring, they grow longer.
   [Combine these sentence-units into a compound sentence.]

   _____

   _____

4. During his lunch hours, Eric plugged away at his novel.
   In his spare time also, he plugged away at it.
   [Combine the shifters into a compound front shifter.]

   _____

   _____

5. The old lady saved jam jars.
She saved the tins from TV dinners.
She saved odd-sized bits of string.
[Combine the three objects into a compound object.]

_____

_____

6. The students became enraged at the class treasurer.
They threatened to impeach him.
[Combine the two predicates into one compound predicate. Be sure
not to use the subject _they_ with the second predicate, or else you
will end up with a compound sentence, rather than with a compound
predicate.]

_____

_____

TASK C

Read the following passage and mark every coordinator you can find
with a +. (The first one has been done for you.)

+
I never saw this great uncle, but I'm supposed to look like him. I grad-
uated from New Haven in 1915, just a quarter of a century after my father,
and a little later I participated in that delayed Teutonic migration known as
the Great War. I enjoyed the counter-raid so* thoroughly that I came back
restless. Instead of being the warm center of the World, the Middle West
now seemed like the ragged edge of the universe—so I decided to go East
and learn the bond business. Everybody I knew was in the bond business, so
I supposed it could support one more single man. All my aunts and uncles
talked it over as if they were choosing a prep school for me, and finally said,
"Why—yes--es," with very grave, hesitant faces. Father agreed to finance me
for a year, and after various delays I came East, in the spring of twenty-two.

* This _so_ is not the coordinator _so_.

The practical thing was to find rooms in the city, but it was a warm season, and I had just left wide lawns and friendly trees, so when a young man at the office suggested that we should take a house together in a commuting town, it sounded like a great idea. He found the house, a weather-beaten cardboard bungalow at eighty a month, but at the last minute the firm ordered him to Washington, and I went out to the country alone.

—from *The Great Gatsby* by
F. Scott Fitzgerald.

TASK D

Write a short paragraph of seven or eight sentences giving your impression of the narrator of the passage that you have just read. (His name is Nick Carraway.) Try to use compound units when you can, in order to avoid short, choppy sentences.

Included Clauses

8.1 Includers

As you learned in Section 7.3, two sentence-units can be joined by a co-ordinator to form a compound sentence. Another way of combining two sentence-units, however, is to "include" or "embed" one of them in the other, usually as a shifter. This can be done by preceding the sentence-unit that is to be embedded with a special kind of word called an **includer.** A fairly complete list of includers appears inside the back cover. Here are a few common ones:

after	before	when	while
because	since	if	although

Many sentence-units can be embedded in other sentence-units in this way. The sentence-unit that is to be embedded, *together with the includer that precedes it,* is called an **included clause.** This included clause is then embedded as either a front shifter or end shifter inside the other sentence-unit.

For example, we can make the first sentence in the following pair an included clause by adding an includer to it:

Mary loved John herself.
Mary didn't give him Sue's message.

We simply add the includer *because* and then "include" the included clause in either the F position or the E position in the other sentence:

            F   T

Because Mary loved John herself,) she didn't give him Sue's message.

            T   E

Mary didn't give John Sue's message(because she loved him herself.

The combined sentence has the same meaning regardless of whether the included clause fills the F or E position. (The other changes—from *Mary* to *she* and from *John* to *him*—are incidental.) Here's another example:

Our team plays basketball well. We never win.

            F   T

Although our team plays basketball well,) we never win.

Notice that an included clause in the F position is usually followed by a comma, although no comma is really needed when the included clause fills the E position. Compare the last example with this one:

            T   E

Our team never wins at basketball(although we play it well.

(Once again, the nouns and pro-nominals have been shifted around so that the nouns will come first, *before* the pro-nominals that refer back to them.)
You should always remember that, once an includer has been added to a sentence-unit, the sentence-unit becomes an *included clause* and *must then be included* as a shifter in a larger sentence-unit. You should not write an included clause as if it were a sentence all by itself.

PRACTICE 1

Combine the following sentence-units (written here as complete sentences) according to the instructions. (The first one has been done for you.)

1. A. Angie couldn't sleep.
   B. She took a sleeping pill.
   [Using the includer *until,* make sentence B into an included clause in the E position.]

   Angie couldn't sleep until she took a sleeping pill.

2. A. Ann was very pleased with herself.
   B. She bought herself a present.
   [Using the includer *because,* make sentence A into a front shifter.
   Don't forget to place a comma after the front shifter.]

_____

3. A. The lions only yawned.
   B. The lion trainer cracked his whip.
   [Using the includer *when,* make sentence B into an end shifter.]

_____

4. A. He got himself a snack.
   B. The commercials were on.
   [Using the includer *while,* make sentence B into a *front* shifter.]

_____

5. A. Bob had heard the joke once.
   B. He had forgotten it.
   [Using the includer *although,* make sentence A into a front shifter.]

_____

8.2 Shifters as Clues to Meaning

The included clauses you have worked with so far were all adverbial clauses. (You will encounter other kinds of included clauses in later units.) Like all adverbial units, adverbial clauses "say something more," usually about the trunks in their sentences; that is to say, they provide *additional* information. The kind of information that an included clause adds is signaled by the includer that introduces the clause.

Time. The most common kind of information that an adverbial clause gives is information about time. Actually, an adverbial clause of time does not always tell the reader just *when* something happened; it is more likely to tell the reader whether one event happened before, after, or at the same time as another event. The includers that show **time-relationships** like these are the includers *after, before, when, while, as* (meaning "while"), *since* (meaning "from an earlier time to the present"), and *until* (or *till*). For example:

F

Before he gets on a plane, Mr. Fields always has several stiff drinks.

F

After he quarreled with his relatives,) the old man changed his will several times.

E

Carol listened to records (**as she did her homework.**

E

The cupboard was bare (**when Mother Hubbard looked in it.**

Cause. Other adverbial clauses tell the reader the *reason* for the predication expressed in the trunk or else explain the *cause* of that predication. The includer *because* is commonly used for this purpose, as are the includers *since* and *as* when they mean "because." For example:

E

The flashlight didn't work (**because the batteries were dead.**

E

No one told Benedict any secrets (**since he was known to be a spy.**

E

The British were disappointed and worried (**as they had received no secret information from Benedict in some time.**

(You will notice that *as* has a rather formal sound when it is used in this way. *Because* and *since* are more common.)

Condition. Sometimes a statement is true only under certain conditions. In such cases, there is usually an included clause in the sentence that tells what those conditions are; such a clause commonly begins with the includer *if* or else with the includer *unless* (which has the meaning "if . . . not"). For example:

F

If he can get five hundred dollars for his car,) he will sell it immediately.

E

His wife threatened to leave him (**unless he stopped watching football all day Sunday. (That is, if he did not stop watching football all day Sunday.)**

Concession. Adverbial clauses introduced by *although*, *even though*, and *while* (when it means "although") give information that seems to go counter to the idea stated in the trunk. These includers signal that the statement is still true, in spite of the fact or facts stated in the shifter. A few examples may make this clearer:

F

Although the Spartans fought bravely,) they were eventually defeated.

E

Joan applied for stewardess training, (**even though she feared flying.**

F

While Benedict seemed loyal enough,) nobody really trusted him with military secrets.

PRACTICE 2

even though	as	before	since
while	after	if	although

Change the first sentence in each of the following pairs into a shifter, using one of the includers listed above. Make up a shifter that will suggest the meaning indicated in the brackets. (The first one has been done.)

1. Joan hates flying.
   She should stop being a stewardess.
   [Under these conditions, the next statement is reasonable.]

   If Joan hates flying, she should stop being a stewardess.
   _____

2. The old miser died.
   His heirs started quarreling over the estate.
   [Use an includer that shows the logical time-relationship between the two statements.]

   _____
   _____

3. I like the white suit better.
   It is less practical than the blue one.
   [Use an includer that suggests that the speaker is going to buy the sensible blue suit.]

   _____
   _____

4. Charlie had broken training one more time.
   He would have been off the team.
   [Use an includer that suggests that Charlie's shaping up was a condition for his staying on the team.]

   _____

5. I am going that way anyway.
   I will give you a lift.
   [Use an includer that suggests that the first statement is a reason for the second.]

8.3 To Compound or to Include?

As you write, you will often have to choose between *compounding,* the method of joining sentences that you studied in Unit 7, and *including,* the method that you have been working with in this unit. In many cases one will be as good as the other. But sometimes choosing one over the other may give additional force or clarity to what you write. Since the choice may be important, it will be worthwhile to stop and compare the kinds of sentences that result from these two different methods of combining.

We will begin by looking at two sentence-units that can be joined in either way:

The Spartans fought bravely.

The Persians captured the pass.

The Spartans were defending the pass, not in the hope of holding it permanently, but in order to gain time. The two sentence-units can be brought together in a compound sentence like this one:

The Spartans fought bravely, but the Persians captured the pass.

Compounding has the effect of giving the sentence-units equal force. The coordinator *but* signals that the statement that follows contrasts in some way with the one that precedes it.

Now compare the compound sentence above with the next one, in which the first sentence-unit is an included clause:

Although the Spartans fought bravely, the Persians captured the pass.

The includer *although* specifies the meaning relationship more clearly than does the coordinator *but* in the compound sentence; at the same time, the includer has the effect of de-emphasizing the feat of the Spartans. The fact that they fought bravely has been made an item of additional information, while the emphasis is on the statement about the Persians.

It is generally true that includers give a more specific clue to the meaning relationship between sentence-units than do coordinators. Therefore, when it is important to show that one statement indicates the cause or condition for the other or when it is important to express the time-relationship between the two statements, an included clause is usually your best bet. But when you want sentence-units to have equal weight, you should usually use a compound sentence.

The examples that follow illustrate some typical situations in which one or the other of these methods of combining would be preferred.

1. While Hilda was waiting for dinner, she ate several sandwiches and a chocolate eclair. [The includer *while* specifies the time-relationship.]
2. Since gasoline is volatile, it is dangerous to store it in your basement. [*Since* signals that the included clause gives a reason in support of the following statement.]
3. Goliath was armed to the teeth; David carried only a slingshot. [The compound sentence gives both parts equal weight and highlights the contrast between the two fighters.]
4. Earlier, King Saul had offered David his own armor, but it was too big for the boy. [Stated in a compound sentence, the two statements have equal weight.]

PRACTICE 3

Now rewrite the numbered sentences above, changing each compound sentence into a sentence with an included clause, and each sentence with an included clause into a compound sentence. Make as few other changes as possible. If you feel that a change in meaning or emphasis is suggested when you combine the sentences differently, try to explain what the change in meaning is. State *for each sentence* which form of combining you think comes closest to bringing out the important ideas.

1. _____

_____

_____

2. _____

_____

_____

3. _____

_____

_____

4. _____

_____

_____

TASK A

Rewrite each of the following pairs of sentences, combining them into one longer sentence. Use an includer at the beginning of one sentence or the other to make it an included clause for use in either the F position or the E position in the other sentence. When you use an included clause in the F position, remember to put a comma after it. (The first pair of sentences has been done for you.)

1. Time is very important in North America.
   It is treated rather casually in Latin America.

   F

   Although time is very important in North America, it is treated rather

   casually in Latin America.

2. You keep a North American waiting more than forty-five minutes.
   You insult him.

   _____

   _____

3. People from different cultures treat time in different ways.
   They often misunderstand each other.

   _____

   _____

4. The way people feel about time varies from culture to culture.
   It is important to know the different languages of time.

   _____

   _____

5. You are a guest in another country.
   You should observe the customs of that country.

   _____

   _____

6. You have learned the customs.
   You will be able to communicate better with the people.

   _____

   _____

TASK B

Each of the following pairs of sentences can be combined in one of two ways: (1) by making one sentence in the pair into a shifter to be included in the other, or (2) by joining both sentences in the pair with a co-ordinator like *and, or, but,* or *so.* Use whichever method you think will make the resulting sentence clearer and better.

1. The dwarfs took the comb out of Snow White's hair.
   She opened her eyes.

   _____

   _____

2. Bill rode his bike into town.
   His car was not working.

   _____

   _____

3. Some people set their goals low.
   They are afraid of failing.

   _____

   _____

4. Columbus wanted to sail on.
   His men were ready to turn back.

   _____

   _____

5. Angie had studied for the exam.
   She was a little nervous about passing it.

   _____

   _____

6. The store was in a good location.
   Business was poor.

_____

_____

TASK C

Read the following passage, underlining and cutting off with parentheses all of the included clauses. Mark each included clause *F* or *E* depending upon whether it is in the front or end position in its own sentence. (Some sentences, of course, may have no included clauses. The first sentence has been marked for you.)

E

The first life on earth evolved in the sea (because conditions there were favorable to it. Although fossils 500 million years old have been found preserved in rock, most earlier forms of life have left no trace since the creatures were soft-bodied and had no hard parts to be preserved.

When the first animals ventured onto land, they took part of the sea with them. Every warm-bodied bird and animal carries in its veins a salty stream made up of sodium, potassium, and calcium in about the same proportions as in sea water. This may be an inheritance from our earliest ancestors, since the first creatures on earth probably had a circulatory system that consisted of sea water.

If life really began in the sea, we all repeat the steps through which living organisms originally evolved. Each of us begins his life in a miniature ocean within his mother's womb. Although the end result is different, every animal and person passes through the same stages. Before an animal is born, it begins as a gill-breathing creature and slowly develops into one that can live on land.

TASK D

Write five sentences of your own, each with an included clause in it, either in the F position or the E position. Try to use a different includer for each included clause. The sentences do not all have to deal with the same idea. You may express five different ideas if you would like to.

One-and-a-Half Sentences

9.1   Half-Sentences

A third way of combining two sentences is by reducing one to a **half-sentence** and then adding it to the other. We will start out by learning how to cut sentences into half-sentences. Then in Section 9.2 we will look at different ways of combining half-sentences and full sentences.

Only certain sentences can be cut "in half," namely, sentences that contain one of the following X-words: *am, is, are, was,* and *were* (or the forms *be* or *been).* To cut a sentence in half, we remove *both the subject and the X-word.* (If either *be* or *been* is used in the sentence, the cut comes after that word.) For example:

half-sentences

	S	X	
	Ⅰ	am	**feeling tired.**
X̃	S		
Are	you		**ready to go home?**
	S	X	
	The boys	were	**playing football in the rain.**

87

```
      S        X
```
The suspect has been **shown the evidence.**

```
     S         X
```
Jimmy   was   **covered with mud.**

As you can see, most half-sentences are predicatids. (Predicatids are described in Section 5.4)

Note that in all of the example sentences above, which have been cut in half by removing the subject and the X-word, the S and X positions (or the X̃ and S positions) come at the very beginning, *before* the half-sentence. Therefore, if we want to cut *a sentence with one or more front shifters* in half, we must first shift all the shifters to the end position, so that the S and X positions will come at the very beginning. For example:

```
        F₁                          F₂
```
Friday afternoon,$)$ in the middle of rush-hour traffic,$)$ the old man was

```
      T
```
crossing Broadway against the light.

```
                     T                              E₁
```
The old man was crossing Broadway against the light$($in the middle of

```
                     E₂
```
rush-hour traffic$($Friday afternoon.

```
      S        X              half-sentence
```
The old man was **crossing Broadway against the light in the middle of rush-hour traffic Friday afternoon.**

Notice that half-sentences are not complete predicates. When we remove the X-word, we remove the signal of time-orientation, which a predicate must have in order to be complete. For instance, the half-sentence *covered with mud* in the next-to-the-last example above can refer to past time. But it can also refer to present time or even to future time:

Jimmy was   covered with mud.   (past)

Jimmy is   covered with mud.   (present)

Jimmy will be   covered with mud.   (future)

By contrast, a complete predicate, *with* an X-word, always shows time-orientation. For instance, *was covered with mud*—the complete predicate in the first of the three examples—can only refer to past time.

Half-sentences are very common in questions and exclamations, where the missing subjects and X-words can easily be supplied:

Ready to go home?

Aha! Smoking again!

Half-sentences also turn up in advertisements. For example:

Baked fresh every morning.

Untouched by human hands.

PRACTICE 1

Make half-sentences out of the sentences that follow by removing the subject and the X-word. (Write only the half-sentences on the blank lines.) One sentence has no X-word in it and cannot be cut "in half" by the method described above. Just leave a blank for that sentence. (The first half-sentence has been written down for you.)

1. He was signed up by the Mets.

   signed up by the Mets
   _____

2. Our product is assembled by elves in the Black Forest.

   _____

3. Somebody is shouting for help.

   _____

4. The movie gets better toward the end.

   _____

5. The lion was showing signs of irritation.

   _____

6. This garment was made by union labor.

   _____

9.2 Adding Half-Sentences

Once a half-sentence has been derived from a full sentence by cutting off the subject and X-word, it can be embedded in another sentence that has the same subject. For example, take these two sentences:

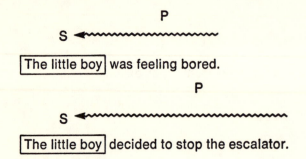

P

S ◄〜〜〜〜〜〜〜〜〜

| The little boy | was feeling bored.

P

S ◄〜〜〜〜〜〜〜〜〜〜〜〜

| The little boy | decided to stop the escalator.

The first sentence can be reduced to a half-sentence by cutting off the subject and X-word:

     S   X *half-sentence*

| The little boy | was **feeling bored.**

The half-sentence can then be embedded in the F position in the other sentence *as a front shifter*, with a comma after it:

                                             P

    F   S ◄〜〜〜〜〜〜〜〜〜〜

Feeling bored, | the little boy | decided to stop the escalator.

This results in a sentence made up of a half-sentence added to a full sentence. We will call this kind of sentence a **one-and-a-half sentence.**

    In Section 9.1 you learned that all front shifters must be shifted to the end position before a sentence can be cut "in half." The end shifters then become part of the half-sentence (even in a one-and-a-half sentence). For example:

                                    F

After two hours of shopping with his mother in a large department

                T

store,〉the little boy was feeling bored.

         T   **E**

The little boy was feeling bored (after two hours of shopping with his mother in a large department store.

         S   **X**   *half-sentence*

1st Sentence: [The little boy] was **feeling bored after two hours of shopping with his mother in a large department store.**

                           P

        S ⟵~~~~~~

2nd Sentence: [The little boy] decided to stop the escalator.

                       F

1½ Sentence: **Feeling bored after two hours of shopping with his mother**

                                P

                  S ⟵~~~~~~~~~~~~~~~~~~~~~~~~~~

in a large department store, [the little boy] **decided to stop** the escalator.

Two sentences can also be combined in a one-and-a-half sentence if the subject of one is a pro-nominal that refers to the subject of the other. The full subject (that is, not the pro-nominal) then becomes the subject in the one-and-a-half sentence. For example:

       S   **X**   *half-sentence*

[The old man] was **crossing Broadway against the light in the middle of rush-hour traffic Friday afternoon.**

               P

    S ⟵~~~~~~~~~~~~~~~~~~~~

[He] was hit by a taxi.

                       F

Crossing Broadway against the light in the middle of rush hour traffic

                       P

        S ⟵~~~~~~~~~~~~~~~~~

Friday afternoon, [the old man] **was hit by a taxi.**

Like the full predicate, the half-sentence also makes a predication about the subject. We can show the difference between these two kinds of predications by marking the "primary predication" (that is, the time-oriented predicate) with a wavy arrow, and the "secondary predication" (the half-sentence) with a broken arrow, both pointing toward the subject:

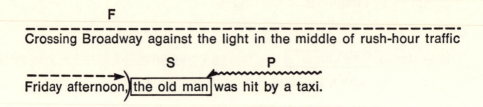

Like other shifters in the F position, half-sentences can also appear in the E position. But unlike the other shifters, this kind of shifter does not always "feel" quite right in the E position. For instance, this sentence sounds all right:

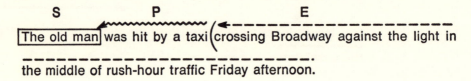

the middle of rush-hour traffic Friday afternoon.

But this one does not:

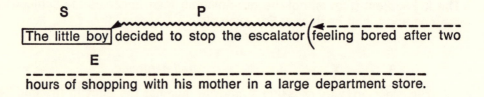

hours of shopping with his mother in a large department store.

This last sentence is not quite un-English enough to mark with an asterisk. It can be made a little better, however, by the addition of a comma before the half-sentence. Indeed, some writers would prefer to have a comma in the first sentence, also:

The little boy decided to stop the escalator, feeling bored after two hours of shopping with his mother in a large department store.

The old man was hit by a taxi, crossing Broadway against the light in the middle of rush-hour traffic Friday afternoon.

But most frequently the half-sentence sounds better in the F position, where it is close to the subject that it makes a predication about.

One other possible position for a half-sentence is immediately after the subject:

      S   **W**

The little boy, feeling bored after two hours of shopping with his

                                              P

mother in a large department store, decided to stop the escalator.

Notice that when a half-sentence is inserted between the subject and predicate of a full sentence, it is set off with a pair of commas. (We will mark this "insert" position between the subject and predicate *W*.)

PRACTICE 2

Make one-and-a-half sentences out of the following pairs of sentences. First check to make sure that both sentences in each pair have subjects that refer to the same person or object. Then make a half-sentence out of the first sentence in each pair by removing the subject and X-word, and rewrite the two sentences as a simple one-and-a-half sentence, with the half-sentence added *in the F position.* (The first one has been done for you.) **Note:** In one pair of sentences the subject is not the same in both sentences. You cannot combine those two sentences into a one-and-a-half sentence. Leave the blank line under the sentences empty.

1. The baby was frightened by the thunder.
   The baby began to cry.

   Frightened by the thunder, the baby began to cry.

2. The tramp steamer was listing badly.
   The tramp steamer limped into port.

   _____

3. Pierre was encouraged by his luck.
   Pierre bet his winnings on a long shot.

   _____

4. The church was begun more than fifty years ago.
   They still have not finished building it.

   _____

5. The floor walker was looking pale.
   The floor walker ushered the little boy out of the store.

   _____

6. Eric was hoping to hear from his publisher.
   Eric kept hanging around the mailbox.

   _____

9.3 ING Forms

As you learned in Section 9.1, half-sentences have no time-orientation. The ones you have worked with so far were made "time-less" by removing the X-word in a sentence (along with the subject). In other words, every half-sentence you have worked with was derived from a sentence that already had an X-word in it (in fact, an X-word of the form *am, is, are, was,* or *were*).

But a half-sentence can also be derived from a sentence that does not have an X-word in it by changing the time-oriented verb in the predicate to its **ING form,** which is *not* time-oriented. Look, for example, at these two sentences:

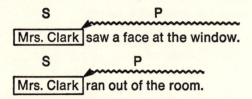

Since both sentences have the same subject, it seems as if it should be possible to combine them into a one-and-a-half sentence. To derive the half-sentence, we must remove the subject of one of the sentences. Since neither sentence has an X-word, we must change the time-oriented verb in one of them to its ING form; that is, we must change *saw* to *seeing* (or else *ran* to *running*). This will give us a half-sentence (either *seeing a face at the window* or *running out of the room*), which we can then embed in the F position in the other sentence. Depending on which half-sentence we choose, we will end up with one or the other of these two one-and-a-half sentences:

F   S   P

Seeing a face at the window, Mrs. Clark ran out of the room.

F   S   P

Running out of the room, Mrs. Clark saw a face at the window.

The first sentence sounds better, since Mrs. Clark probably saw the face before she ran out. We will therefore choose the first sentence as the better one-and-a-half sentence. (Sometimes both sentences put together in this way will sound equally good. You will then have to choose the one you like better—the one that comes nearer to saying what you want to say.)

The half-sentence could of course be shifted from the F position to the E position. For example:

    S   P   E

Mrs. Clark ran out of the room, seeing a face at the window.

But again, our first choice is probably the better one since Mrs. Clark's seeing the face at the window preceded in time her running out of the room.

All of this may sound rather complicated, but from this discussion you should at least be able to get some idea of the great variety of sentences you can choose from. Half-sentences make it possible to "pack" sentences with two (or even more) ideas in any of several different ways. For example, by using both the F and E positions, we can embed two half-sentences in a larger sentence. Both half-sentences, however, must make predications about the subject of the full sentence. For example:

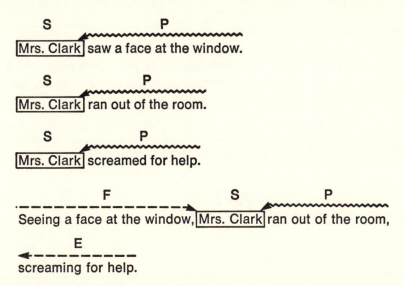

Unlike other half-sentences, those made with ING forms can be used after includers and even after prepositions (that is, after words like *on, in, by, with, for, of,* etc.). For example:

                             F   S

While walking to the center of the stage, the young rock singer waved

    P

to the audience.

                                   F   S   P
‑‑‑‑‑‑‑‑‑‑‑‑‑‑‑‑‑‑‑‑‑‑‑‑‑‑‑▶
On reaching the center of the stage, ⃞he⃞ grasped the microphone.

                              F   S   P
‑‑‑‑‑‑‑‑‑‑‑‑‑‑‑‑‑‑‑‑‑‑‑▶
After grasping the microphone, ⃞he⃞ began to sing.

Remember that you can make up one-and-a-half sentences by the methods described in this unit only *when the subjects of the original sentences are the same* (or refer to the same person or object).

As a kind of review, let's look now at three different kinds of half-sentences and see how we can embed them in the F and E positions (and in the W position just after the subject) in a long sentence, to make it longer.

                    S   X
⃞The young rock singer⃞ was **dressed in a pink satin shirt and purple**

jeans.

⃞He⃞ was **aware that every eye in the hall was on him.**

⃞He⃞ smiled shyly at the audience.

We can insert the three sentences above as half sentences into the sentence below, in order to form one really long sentence that expresses *five* ideas:

       F   S   W   P   +
‑‑‑▶ ⟩⃞The young rock singer,⃞ walked to the center of the stage and

                                              E
〜〜〜〜〜〜〜〜〜〜〜〜〜⟨◀‑‑‑
grasped the microphone.⟨

                                    F   S
‑‑‑‑‑‑‑‑‑‑‑‑‑‑‑‑‑‑‑‑‑‑‑‑▶
Dressed in a pink satin shirt and purple jeans, ⃞the young rock singer,⃞

◀‑‑‑‑‑‑‑‑‑‑W‑‑‑‑‑‑‑‑‑‑‑ ◀〜〜〜P〜〜〜
aware that every eye in the hall was on him, walked to the center

              +   E
〜〜〜〜〜〜〜〜〜〜〜〜〜〜〜〜◀‑‑‑‑‑‑‑‑‑‑‑‑
of the stage and grasped the microphone, smiling shyly at the au-

‑‑‑‑.
dience.

PRACTICE 3

Make the first sentence in each pair below into a half-sentence by re-moving the subject and changing the time-oriented verb to its ING form. Then embed the half-sentence in the F or E position in the other sentence. (The first one has been done for you.)

1. The rock singer walked to the mike.
    He smiled shyly at the audience.

    (Half-sentence)   walking to the mike.

    (1½ sentence)   Walking to the mike, the rock singer smiled

    shyly at the audience.

2. His fans roared in anticipation.
    They greeted him with cheers and screams.

    (Half-sentence)

    (1½ sentence)

3. The heroine squirmed on the track.
    She helplessly watched the approaching express.

    (Half-sentence)

    (1½ sentence)

4. Lefty bobbed skillfully.
    He awaited an opening.

    (Half-sentence)

    (1½ sentence)

5. Clara thought the piece was over.
    She began to applaud loudly.

    (Half-sentence)

    (1½ sentence)

TASK A

Combine each of the following pairs of sentences by making one of the sentences in each pair into a half-sentence and then embedding the half-sentence in the F, W, or E position in the other sentence. Mark the X positions, and use a slash mark to separate the subject and X-word from the half-sentence. (The first two pairs of sentences have been done for you.) **Note:** First check to make sure that both sentences in each pair make predications about *the same subject.* For any pair of sentences with *different* subjects, you will have to change one of the sentences into *an included clause* before you can embed it in the other sentence.

          X

1. Andrew Wyeth is/considered one of the best contemporary American artists.
   He is famous for his paintings of local people in local settings.

                    F

(1½ sentence)   Considered one of the best contemporary American

artists,⟩ Andrew Wyeth is famous for his paintings of local people in

local settings.

          X

2. Andrew Wyeth is/one of the best of contemporary American painters.
   He is famous for his paintings of local people in local settings.

                    W

(1½ sentence)   Andrew Wyeth, one of the best of contemporary

American painters, is famous for his paintings of local people in

local settings.

3. Wyeth spends his summers in Cushing, Maine.
   His winters are spent in Chadds Ford, Pennsylvania.

(1½ Sentence) _____

_____

_____

4. *Christina's World* is known as one of Wyeth's most famous paintings. It was painted at the farm of Christina and Alvaro Olson in Maine.

(1½ Sentence) _____

_____

_____

5. Christina Olson was crippled and unable to leave her farm. Christina Olson was a tragic figure.

(1½ Sentence) _____

_____

_____

6. *Christina's World* represents the limited world of Christina Olson. [Since there is no X-word, you will have to change the verb to its ING form.]
Christina's World aptly illustrates Wyeth's own world, which he limits to Maine and Pennsylvania.

(1½ Sentence) _____

_____

_____

7. Wyeth seems to be particularly fond of the color white. White appears frequently in his landscapes with fallen snow.

(1½ Sentence) _____

_____

_____

8. Wyeth is especially interested in depicting local people. Wyeth has painted many portraits of his family and of neighbors.

(1½ Sentence) _____

_____

_____

TASK B

Combine each of the following pairs of sentences by making one of the two sentences in each pair into a half-sentence and then embedding the half-sentence in the F, W, or E position in the other sentence. Write the one-and-a-half sentence that you have created on the blank line below each pair. *Be sure that both sentences make predications about the same subject before you combine them in a one-and-a-half sentence.* (The first pair of sentences has been combined for you.)

1. Old coats, boots, and hats are often used as the main subjects of Wyeth's paintings.
   They reflect the artist's love of costume.

   Often used as the main subjects of Wyeth's paintings, old coats,

   boots, and hats reflect the artist's love of costume.

2. A wainscot chair is draped with a duplicate of George Washington's coat.
   A wainscot chair seems to have the General himself sitting on it.

   _____

   _____

3. Wyeth's love of costume is an interesting contrast to his love of nature.
   It is beautifully reflected in his painting *The General's Chair.*

   _____

   _____

4. The artist's wife is depicted in costume in the painting *Maga's Daughter.*
   She is wearing a black silk dress and a broad-brimmed hat.

   _____

   _____

5. Two pale blue streamers are hanging from either side of the crown.
   They make Betsy Wyeth's hat seem less austere.

   _____

   _____

6. A soft brown felt hat is present in many of Wyeth's paintings of his wife Betsy.
   It seems to symbolize the gentleness of her nature.

   _____

   _____

7. Many intimate details fill Wyeth's paintings.
   His paintings convey a multitude of human feelings and attitudes.

   _____

   _____

8. Many of Wyeth's paintings are exhibited at the Museum of Fine Arts in Boston.
   They can also be seen in a book entitled *Andrew Wyeth,* which contains reproductions of his works.

   _____

   _____

TASK C

Find the half-sentences in the following passage and mark them with a broken arrow pointing toward the subject. Draw a box around each subject and label it *S*.

                                                                S
- - - - - - - - - - - - - - - - - - →
Example: While studying medicine at Cornell, [Janet] became interested in acupuncture.

Little known in the West until recently, the Chinese art of acupuncture has become a subject of great interest. Involving the puncture of the patient's skin with gold or silver needles, acupuncture is used to cure diseases, relieve pain, and anesthetize. Some American doctors are now studying this ancient art, believing that they may be able to supplement their own knowledge and skills.

The main problem in studying acupuncture results from the fact that the ancient writings on the subject may be interpreted in many different ways. Dating back to the fourteenth century B.C., writings on acupuncture contain ideographs, or "picture words," for diseases and procedures. Having changed somewhat in meaning over the centuries, the ideographs are sometimes difficult to interpret. Modern scholars, now studying these ancient writings, hope to learn still more secrets of this ancient art.

TASK D

Write three pairs of sentences. Make sure that the two sentences in each pair have the same subject. Then combine the two sentences into a one-and-a-half sentence. You can make either member of the pair into a half-sentence, and you can put the half-sentence in the F, W, or E position in the other sentence. But be sure that your final sentence sounds natural.

Making
Connections

10.1 Connecting Sentences

In the last several units we have been working with various ways of packing more information into individual sentences. Most of these ways involve combining two or more sentences into a single full sentence. In this unit, we will be reviewing some of these combining methods, with the idea of selecting the one that is most effective in a particular situation.

But first there is one more set of connectives that you have to know about. These connectives, called **linkers,** do not join parts of sentences, like the coordinators or the includers. Instead, a linker usually provides a transition from one sentence to another.

Some common linkers, such as *and, but, or,* or *so,* are also coordinators. We will call them linkers when they are used to make *a connection in meaning* between two sentences. When they are used in this way, these linkers come at the very beginning of their sentences and "link" their own sentences to the sentences preceding them. (We can mark the position for linkers with a capital *L.*) For example:

The shipwrecked sailors eventually hoped to find a way of getting off

L

Deadman's Island. **But** their immediate concern was finding food, water,

and some kind of shelter.

Using either *but, and, or,* or *so* as a linker at the beginning of a sentence to "link" the sentence to the preceding sentence gives both sentences more emphasis than they would have as parts of a compound sentence. But like all kinds of emphasis, this one loses its effectiveness when it is used too often.

A few other linkers, which are also used in the L position to link their sentences to preceding sentences are *yet, next, then, now, finally, as a result, for that reason, in other words, on the other hand,* and *as a matter of fact.* Here are some examples of their use:

For days Eric hung around the mailbox waiting for some reaction to

L

the novel he had sent off to his publisher. **Finally,** the postman brought

him a letter.

The bank teller tactfully told Fran that her account was underdeposited.

L

In other words, Fran's account was overdrawn.

L

The Penguins are a good hockey team. **As a matter of fact,** they have

won the city cup for the last three years.

There is a special set of linkers, which we will call **roving linkers,** that are also used to link their own sentences to preceding sentences. A roving linker may appear in the L position, or else it may be used as an insert at any borderline between two positions. As an insert, it is usually set off from the rest of its own sentence by a comma (or two commas). The roving linkers include *however, therefore, furthermore, nevertheless,* and *consequently.* Here are examples showing how a roving linker can "rove" from the L position to almost any borderline between two positions, right up to the very end of the sentence.

L

However, a careful writer should avoid using linkers in every sentence.

S   X

A careful writer, *however,* should avoid using linkers in every sentence.

X   V

A careful writer should, *however,* avoid using linkers in every sentence.

A careful writer should avoid using linkers in every sentence, *however.*

PRACTICE 1

From the examples given above, choose an appropriate linker to insert in the blank in the following sentences in order to make a smooth connection in meaning between the preceding and following sentences.

1. Mr. O'Brien worked hard all his life and saved every penny he could.

   _____, he would have died poor if a long lost uncle had not left him half a million dollars.

2. The builder had underestimated the cost of materials and the length

   of time required to put up a building. _____, he lost his shirt.

3. He had looked forward for weeks to getting this particular letter.

   The letter itself, _____, was something of a disappointment.

4. At the present time, mass production of the automobile engine you invented that burns only gin or vodka does not seem practical.

   _____, if gasoline prices continue to rise, we may wish to reconsider.

5. Angie had studied tap dancing for years. _____, her big break came when a talent scout heard her singing a solo with the school chorus.

6. The detective expected the butler to answer his knock. _____

   _____, he was surprised when Lady Fogbottom opened the door herself.

10.2 Connecting Ideas

By now you have practiced various ways of building (and packing) mature sentences, connecting the ideas within a sentence, or linking one sentence to another. The tasks that follow are to help you review some of these skills in combination. At various places in the instructions, you will see numbers like "§ 9.1" or "§ 7.2." These references are to sections in this book in which you will find explanations and examples that may help you to solve a particular problem. Be sure to go back and review each such section if you need to.

TASK A

Combine the following pairs of sentences according to the bracketed instructions. The relevant section number will help you to review the steps involved, in case you do not remember all of them.

1. Craven isn't the starting quarterback any more.
   He can't remember the signals.
   [Make the second sentence into an included clause and embed it in the *E* position of the first sentence. (§ 8.1)]

   _____

   _____

2. The candidate refused to concede.
   The candidate demanded a recount.
   [Use a coordinator to form a compound predicate. (§ 7.2)]

   _____

   _____

3. [Now go back and make a half-sentence of the first sentence in 2 above and embed it in any suitable position in the other sentence. (§ 9.3)]

   _____

   _____

4. People from other cultures may use many polite expressions in their speech.
   They may give the impression of rudeness because of their use of a different kind of nonverbal communication from the kind we are accustomed to.

   [(a) First, combine these two sentences in a compound sentence, using a suitable coordinator. (b) Then make the first sentence into an included clause and embed it in the *F* position in the second sentence. (§ 8.1)]

   (a) _____

   _____

   (b) _____

   _____

5. [(a) Now go back and write the two sentences in 4 separately again, but insert an appropriate linker in the L position in the second one. (§ 10.1) (b) Then write the second sentence again, with a roving linker in some position other than the L position. (§ 10.1)]

(a) _____

_____

(b) _____

_____

6. The witness was faced with the prospect of a perjury indictment. The witness changed his story.
[Make the first sentence into a half-sentence and embed it in the F position in the second sentence. Then rewrite your one-and-a-half sentence with the half-sentence in the *W* position. (§ 9.2) Which one-and-a-half sentence do you like better?]

_____

_____

7. Central Park is always crowded on weekends.
The Bronx Zoo is always crowded on weekends.
[Rewrite as a single sentence with a compound subject. (§ 7.1)]

_____

_____

8. Jasper was angry at not winning a prize.
He grabbed his diploma.
He stalked out of the auditorium.
He did not even bother to speak to his friends near the door.
[Make the first sentence into a half-sentence and embed it in the F position below. Next, combine the second and third sentences into a single trunk *with a compound predicate.* And finally, make the fourth sentence into a half-sentence and embed it in the E position below. (Your half-sentence will begin with the word *not*. You will have to change the verb *bother* to its ING form.) (§ 9.3)]

_____

_____

_____

TASK B

1. Write two sentences that can be combined either (a) by making one into an included clause to be included in the other (§ 8.1) or (b) by using a coordinator between the two (§ 7.3). Put a check mark in the margin beside the version you think most effective.

(The two sentences) _____

_____

(a) _____

_____

(b) _____

_____

2. Write two sentences, using an appropriate roving linker in the second (§ 10.1). Then rewrite the second sentence, with the roving linker in a different position.

(The two sentences) _____

_____

(The second sentence rewritten) _____

_____

3. Write a sentence with a *compound predicate.* Be sure that the second part of the compound predicate does *not* have its own subject; both parts of the predicate should go with the same subject. (§ 7.2)

_____

_____

Now add either a *front shifter* or an *end shifter* to your sentence with the compound predicate.

_____

_____

And finally, rewrite your sentence, repeating the subject so that you now have a *compound sentence-unit,* with either a front shifter or an end shifter (or both) in one of the two parts. (§ 7.3).

_____

_____

4. Write two sentences with the same subject. Then make one into a half-sentence and embed it in the other. (§§ 9.2-3)

(The two sentences) _____

_____

(The one-and-a-half sentence) _____

_____

5. Write a sentence that has one half-sentence in the F position and one in the E position. Begin with three sentences that have the same subject. (§ 9.3) Mark the F and E positions in the final sentence.

(Sentence 1) _____

(Sentence 2) _____

(Sentence 3) _____

(The final sentence) _____

_____

TASK C

Underline all linkers in the following passage.

The knights had now lost their tempers and the battle was joined in earnest. It did not matter much, however, for they were so encased in metal that they could not do each other much damage. It took them so long to get up, and the dealing of a blow when you weighed the eighth part of a ton was such a cumbrous business, that every stage of the contest could be marked and pondered.

In the first stage King Pellinore and Sir Grummore stood opposite each other for about half an hour, and walloped each other on the helm. There was only opportunity for one blow at a time, so they more or less took it in turns, King Pellinore striking while Sir Grummore was recovering, and vice versa. At first, if either of them dropped his sword or got it stuck in the ground, the other put in two or three extra blows while he was patiently fumbling for it or trying to tug it out. Later, they fell into the rhythm of the thing more perfectly, like the toy mechanical people who saw wood on Christmas trees. Eventually the exercise and the monotony restored their good humour and they began to get bored.

The second stage was introduced as a change, by common consent. Sir Grummore stumped off to one end of the clearing, while King Pellinore plodded off to the other. Then they turned round and swayed backward and forward once or twice, in order to get their weight on their toes. When they leaned forward they had to run forward, to keep up with their weight, and if they leaned too far backward they fell down. So even walking was complicated. When they had got their weight properly distributed in front of them, so that they were just off their balance, each broke into a trot to keep up with himself. They hurtled together as it had been two boars.

They met in the middle, breast to breast, with a noise of shipwreck and great bells tolling, and both, bouncing off, fell breathless on their backs. They lay thus for a few minutes, panting. Then they slowly began to heave themselves to their feet, and it was obvious that they had lost their tempers once again.

—From *The Once and Future King*
by T. H. White

TASK D

Write three paragraphs similar to the ones given above in which you describe an event you have witnessed or one you have imagined, involving sequential actions. Be sure to use linkers to tie your sentences together, but try not to rely on them too heavily. Use the selection from above as a guide.

Noun Clusters

11.1 The Nucleus of a Noun Cluster

All subjects and objects (and some complements) are nominals. In this unit and the one that follows, you will be working with a kind of nominal called a **noun cluster.** As you will see, noun clusters provide a very good way of packing additional meaning into a sentence. They are, therefore, worth taking some time with.

A noun cluster consists of a noun, which is the **nucleus** of the cluster, and its **modifiers.** The function of a modifier is to identify the noun in the nucleus or to distinguish the person or thing the noun names from others in the same class. For instance, the noun *girl* can refer to any girl. Modifiers help to show which girl you are talking about:

	girl
a	girl
the	girl
the	girl **on the magazine cover**
the beautiful	girl
the friendly looking	girl

The units in boldface are modifiers. The noun *girl* is the nucleus in each example.

We will mark a noun cluster by placing the symbol ⟨ before it and the symbol ⟩ after it. We will mark the nucleus of the cluster by putting an asterisk (*) under it, and each modifier by drawing an arrow under it pointing toward the nucleus.

Ϩ our house Ϩ

Ϩ the late show Ϩ

Ϩ the first house on the left Ϩ

Ϩ people Ϩ

As you can see from the examples, a noun cluster can consist of a nucleus alone (for instance *people* in the sentence *People are funny*) or a nucleus with one or more modifiers before or after it. Notice also that a group of words like *on the left* functions as a single modifier.

One more thing: A noun cluster sometimes has more than one noun in it. For instance, in this example the noun *snow* is used as a modifier of the noun *tires*

Ϩ the snow tires Ϩ

An easy way to find the nucleus of a cluster like that is to consider what word you would use in a telegram—that is, to decide which noun cannot be left out. A garage owner might wire his supplier:

SHIP TIRES AT ONCE.

If he has already ordered, the supplier should know what kind of tires he wants. But he would obviously not wire

SHIP SNOW AT ONCE.

When you are in doubt about which noun is the nucleus, send yourself a telegram.

PRACTICE 1

Place the symbols (Ϩ Ϩ) around each of the noun clusters below. Then find the nucleus and mark it with an asterisk. Mark each modifier by drawing an arrow under it pointing toward the asterisk. (The first one has been done for you.)

1. Ϩ my favorite television show Ϩ

2. six little green men from Mars

3.   elephants

4.   our annual trip to Duluth

5.   seventy-six trombones

6.   the winner of the essay contest

7.   black olives

8.   his brand-new red convertible with black and white upholstery

9.   twelve long-stemmed red roses

10. the junior senator from Missouri

11.2   Adjectivals and Intensifiers

There are several different kinds of noun modifiers. Perhaps the most important are the **determiners,** which are words like *the, a,* and *an* (sometimes called **articles**), and *my, your, its, his, her, our, their, this, these, that, those, every, some,* and *no.* Words like these help us to "determine" or identify nouns; if we want a person to repeat a noun, for example, we often use a determiner followed by the question-word *what* (or possibly *who*): "His what?" "His advice." "The what?" "The birds."

Other kinds of noun modifiers are **numerals** (as in *two* books), **adjectives** (as in *new* books), and other nouns (as in *history* books). But since adjectives are the most numerous of all modifiers, we will call all noun modifiers **adjectivals**—that is, "adjective-like modifiers."

"Ordinary" adjectives are adjectives like *beautiful, large,* and *blue,* which either can take the endings *-er* and *-est* (e.g., *larger, largest)* or else can be used after *more* and *most* (e.g., *more beautiful, most beautiful).* Ordinary adjectives—and sometimes also adjectives of origin or nationality, like *French*—can almost always be used after words like *very, rather, quite,* and *fairly.* We can say, for example, *very beautiful, very large, very round, very blue*—and even *very French*—but not **very two* or **very history.*

We will call words like *very, rather,* and *fairly,* **intensifiers.** They are used to modify, or "intensify," other modifiers such as adjectives and adverbs: for example, *very large, very slowly, very carefully.* An adjective with its own intensifier functions as a single adjectival (that is, as a single noun modifier) in a noun cluster. For example:

〈six very beautiful, very large glass ink bottles〉

There is a fairly fixed order in which adjectivals can occur in a noun cluster. But if you are a native speaker of English, you will usually not have to think about which one goes before another—the right order will sound natural to you. (For instance *very large glass ink bottles* sounds natural, but **very large ink glass bottles* does not.) If you have trouble finding the right order for the adjectivals in the following exercise, speak to your instructor about it in order to get some extra help.

PRACTICE 2

Each group of short sentences below contains a noun and several adjectivals that can modify it. Combine the noun and the adjectivals into a single noun cluster. Make sure that the whole noun cluster sounds natural when you read it aloud. Then mark each item in the cluster appropriately. (The first one has been done for you.)

1. Her umbrella is yellow. It is small.

    〈 her small yellow umbrella 〉
    ➡   ➡   ➡   *

   _____

2. There are six bottles. They are for perfume. They are very fragile.

   _____

3. That box is made of cardboard. It is rather large. It is brown. It is used for shoes.

   _____

4. Our cook is German. She cooks pastry. She is new.

   _____

5. Your cousins are Canadian. There are two of them. They are very friendly.

   _____

6. Those stories are exciting. They are English. There are two stories. They are mystery stories.

   _____

7. The rolls are fresh. There are a dozen of them. They are from the bakery.

   _____

8. That movie is Italian. It is new. It is popular.

   _____

11.3 Possessives

You will remember that determiners like *my, his,* and *her* are one kind of adjectival. (These and other determiners are discussed in Section 11.2.) For instance, we can have a noun cluster like this:

〈 his new house 〉

But suppose we want to be more specific about whose house we are talking about, as in this sentence:

My brother's new house is air conditioned.

The noun cluster is

〈 my brother's new house 〉

But how should we mark the modifiers? At first glance, we might be inclined to mark *my* with a separate arrow, as we did *his* in the example above. But, on second thought, it becomes clear that *my* does not go with *house;* it is not *my* house, it is *my brother's.* In other words, the determiner position in this noun cluster is filled by the construction *my brother's,* not by the word *my* alone:

〈 my brother's new house 〉

〈 his   new house 〉

As the examples show, *my brother's* fills the determiner position in just the same way that *his* does.

If you look closely at the construction *my brother's,* you will see that it is itself a noun cluster with the ending *'s* added on:

〈 my brother's 〉

So, in this sentence we have one noun cluster used to modify another:

〈 My brother's new house is air conditioned. 〉

We will call constructions like *my brother's* **possessives.** Possessives regularly fill the determiner position in larger noun clusters.

A possessive may consist of more than just a determiner and a noun. It may include one or more additional adjectival modifiers before its own noun nucleus, as in

〈 my oldest brother's new house 〉

115

On the other hand, a possessive may consist of a single noun with no modifier:

Ҟ [David]'s new house Ҟ

When the nominal in a possessive is plural, the nucleus noun commonly ends in *-s.* To form the possessive of such a nominal, we add only an apostrophe ('), not an apostrophe + *s* ('*s*); this makes it possible to avoid having two *s*'s, one after the other:

Ҟ [my parents]' apartment   **not** * [my parents]'s apartment Ҟ

After a one-syllable name ending in *-s* however, some writers add '*s* to form the possessive, while others add only an apostrophe:

either Ҟ[Charles]'s house   **or** Ҟ[Charles]' house Ҟ

The possessive ending is sometimes added to a noun in a phrase following the nucleus in a nominal, rather than to the nucleus itself. For example, *the Queen of England's crown.* We would analyze this noun cluster as follows:

Ҟ [the Queen of England]'s crown Ҟ

The possessive ending is usually added to only the last noun in a compound noun cluster, not to both nouns:

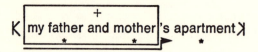

Ҟ [my father and mother]'s apartment Ҟ

In the noun cluster *my brother's new house,* the possessive *my brother's* is made up, as we have seen, of the nominal *my brother* plus the possessive ending '*s*. The substitute for the nominal *my brother* would be the pro-nominal *he;* the substitute for the possessive *my brother's* is the determiner *his:*

PRACTICE 3

Combine the pairs of sentences below by changing the first sentence into a noun cluster introduced by a possessive. Then use the noun cluster as the subject of the second sentence. Follow the example.

Example: My parents have an apartment. It was robbed.

My parents' apartment was robbed.

1. The suspect had an alibi. The alibi was proven false.

2. The new play was written by Smith and Dale. It is a hit.

3. The old orange sweater belongs to Bess. It came unraveled.

4. The dancers made many graceful movements. The movements blended with the music.

5. The Board of Education made a decision. It was unanimous.

TASK A

Some of the noun clusters in the sentences below have been under-lined. Rewrite each of the underlined clusters in the spaces provided below and mark them with the cluster markers (Ҟ Ҡ). Then mark the modifiers and the nucleus in each cluster with arrows and an asterisk. Follow the example.

Example: The Australian aborigines are Stone Age people.

(Cluster)   Ҟ the Australian aborigines Ҡ

1. The Australian continent is the sole dwelling place of these dark-skinned people.

(Cluster)

117

2. <u>These hardy people</u> live in the central deserts which occupy over one-third of the land area of Australia.

   (Cluster)

3. <u>The desert dwellers</u> are a hunting and food-gathering people.

   (Cluster)

4. <u>Crop farming</u> is unknown to them.

   (Cluster)

5. <u>These nomadic people</u> have no permanent camps.

   (Cluster)

6. <u>Their possessions</u> are limited to the bare essentials.

   (Cluster)

7. <u>The men</u> own little more than spears, shields, and boomerangs.

   (Cluster)

8. <u>Most women</u> possess only the necessary utensils for cooking, digging, and grinding.

   (Cluster)

9. Ceremonies make up a major part of <u>the aborigines' life.</u>

   (Cluster)

10. <u>Their elaborate religious rituals</u> commemorate the origin of their world.

    (Cluster)

TASK B

Draw a rectangle around the subject in each of the numbered sentences below and write the subject on the blank line below it between cluster marks. Then analyze the subject cluster, marking its nucleus with an asterisk and marking each of the adjectival modifiers in it with an arrow pointing toward the asterisk. Next draw a rectangle around the nominal in the possessive; and on the line below it, rewrite the nominal as a cluster, between cluster marks, first cutting off the -'s (-', in the case of plural possessives). Finally, analyze that cluster, marking it as you have been marking other clusters. (The first subject has been analyzed for you.)

S

1. A dolphin's fin is made of very strong muscle fiber.

(Subject cluster) ⟨ a dolphin's fin ⟩
⟶ *

(Possessive) a dolphin 's

(Possessive nominal) ⟨ a dolphin ⟩
▶ *

2. A man's best sea friend is the dolphin.

(Subject cluster) _____

(Possessive) _____

(Poss. nom.) _____

3. These creatures' greatest delight is to be able to help man when he is in trouble at sea.

(Subject cluster) _____

(Possessive) _____

(Poss. nom.) _____

4. The dolphin's speed is three times faster than is mathematically possible for the size of its body.

(Subject cluster) _____

(Possessive) _____

(Poss. nom.) _____

5. The sea's warmest currents are what dolphins follow.

(Subject cluster) _____

(Possessive) _____

(Poss. nom.) _____

6. The Navy's technicians are studying the sonar system of dolphins to learn how to improve their own.

(Subject cluster) _____

(Possessive) _____

(Poss. nom.) _____

TASK C

In the following paragraph, some of the words are underlined. If an underlined word is part of a noun cluster, draw a box around the entire cluster. If an underlined word functions as a nominal all by itself, draw a box around the single word. If that word is a noun, write an asterisk under it. If it is a pro-nominal, do not mark it in any way.

Many ancient stories tell about dolphins' aid to men. Up to recent times, however, most people thought that they were myths. During World War II, a dolphin pushed six American aviators in a dinghy to a tiny island. Dolphins have rescued or guided men on numerous occasions. And never has a dolphin attacked a man, even when that man was hunting him. Like man, dolphins are warm-blooded, air-breathing mammals. Could it be that dolphins and men are descended from a common ancestor?

When you have finished, count the number of noun clusters that you have drawn boxes around; the number of single nouns; and the number of pro-nominals. Write the numbers in these blanks:

_____ noun clusters _____ single nouns _____ pro-nominals

TASK D

Write a paragraph about an animal or pet that you have owned (or would like to own). Try to use several noun clusters and at least one pro-nominal and one single noun as nominals in your paragraph.

Expanding
Noun Clusters

12.1 Adjectival Phrases

As you have seen, nominals have many uses in sentences. They can be subjects, objects of verbs, predicators, and modifiers of other nominals. Nominals may also occur after a preposition:

> *prep.*
> of   the new Spanish teacher

We will call a construction like this one a **prepositional phrase**—or simply a **phrase.** The nominal in a phrase is called the **object of the preposition.**
    We will mark a phrase by placing the symbol < before it and the symbol > after it; we will mark the position for the preposition with a small *p* and the position for the object of the preposition with the letters *pO*. We will draw a rectangle around the object to show that it is a nominal:

>   p   pO
> < of [the new Spanish teacher] >

We have already seen phrases used in the F and E positions.

>   F   T
> Without any warning,) Dr. Day's car suddenly stopped.

>   p   pO
> *Phrase:*   < without [any warning] >

                T   E
The motor went dead(because of a faulty generator.

                        p   pO
Phrase: < because of |a faulty generator| >

(Note that the preposition *because of* is made up of two words.)

    Phrases like those in the last two examples above may be called *adverbial* phrases since they fill adverbial positions. But phrases can also be used to fill *adjectival* positions in noun clusters. The position for an adjectival phrase is *after* the noun nucleus, as in the following example:

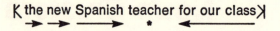

    As you know, a noun cluster like this one can fill the S position in a trunk. For example:

                        S   P
|The new Spanish teacher for our class| will arrive tomorrow.

Since every subject is a nominal, the whole noun cluster *the new Spanish teacher for our class* must be a nominal. As a nominal, it can be used as the object of a preposition. This means that one prepositional phrase can have another phrase embedded inside it. For example:

              V   O
Do you know |the name of the new Spanish teacher for our class?|

Cluster: Kthe name of the new Spanish teacher for our class)

                        p   pO
Phrase: < of |the new Spanish teacher for our class| >

Cluster: K the new Spanish teacher for our class)

                                        p   pO
Phrase: < for |our class| >

Cluster: Kour class)

One of the primary functions of a modifier of a noun, as you learned in the last unit, is to help to identify the referent of the noun. If you saw two women in a doctor's office, one sitting on the couch and one sitting in an armchair, you could use the phrase *on the couch* (or *in the armchair*) to identify the woman you wanted to talk about. For example:

S   P

⎡The woman on the couch⎤ has been waiting for over an hour.

Cluster: 〈 the woman on the couch 〉

         p pO

Phrase: < on ⎡the couch⎤ >

PRACTICE 1

Find the phrase in each sentence below and mark the noun cluster of which it is a part. Then rewrite the phrase in the space below the sentence, marking the preposition and its object. Follow the example.

         S

Example: ⎡A man in a raincoat⎤ is following you.

       p pO

(Phrase) < in ⎡a raincoat⎤ >

1. The murder of Lord Fogbottom shocked London.

   (Phrase)

2. An inspector from Scotland Yard was hastily summoned.

   (Phrase)

3. The police suspected the wife of the murder victim.

   (Phrase)

4. A single diamond earring provided the final clue to the solution.

   (Phrase)

5. Mystery stories with clever solutions are my favorites.

   (Phrase)

12.2   Adjectival Predicatids

Another kind of adjectival modifier which regularly comes after the nucleus in a noun cluster is the predicatid. A predicatid, you will remember, always contains a time-less verb form. Instead of the phrase *on the couch,* for instance, you could use the predicatid *sitting on the couch,* to identify the woman you want to refer to. (From now on, we will mark a predicatid by placing the symbols ⟨ and ⟩ before and after it.) For example:

S

The woman sitting on the couch has been waiting for over an hour.

Cluster: ⟨ the woman sitting on the couch ⟩

Predicatid: ⟨sitting on the couch⟩

If there happened to be two women sitting on the couch instead of only one and if one of the two happened to be reading a magazine, you could identify the woman you want to refer to by using *both* a phrase *and* a predicatid:

S

The woman on the couch reading a magazine has been waiting for over an hour.

Cluster: ⟨ the woman ⟨ on the couch ⟩ ⟨reading a magazine⟩ ⟩

PRACTICE 2

Find the phrase in each sentence below, and mark it off with the phrase markers ⟨ ⟩. Then rewrite the sentence with the phrase changed to a predicatid. Mark the predicatid with the marks ⟨ and ⟩. Follow the example.

Example: My mother is the woman ⟨with the red hat. ⟩

My mother is the woman ⟨wearing the red hat⟩.

1. The man at the center table is the guest speaker.

_____

2. The man at the door is a salesman.

_____

3. Please hand me that notebook on my desk.

_____

4. The woman behind Angie looks familiar.

_____

5. The large painting near the window is a Rembrandt.

_____

12.3 Adjectival Clauses

In Unit 8, you worked with included clauses that give additional information about the trunk of a sentence. In this example, the included clause is in boldface type:

Mr. Micawber couldn't pay his bills **because he had no money.**

This kind of clause is adverbial because it adds something more to the statement made in the trunk—in this case, by giving a reason.

A clause can also be embedded or included in a nominal to identify the person or thing referred to by the nominal. A clause used in this way is called an **adjectival clause.** An adjectival clause is usually introduced by the includer *that* or a WH word—*who, which,* or *whose.* For example:

An American river **that flows north** is the Red River.

An American river **which flows north** is the Red River.

A person **that can foretell the future** is a prophet.

A person **who can foretell the future** is a prophet.

As the examples suggest, there are conventions in edited English that govern the choice of the includer. *Which* is used for anything *except* people; *who* is used only for people; and *that* is used for either people or things. *Whose,* the possessive form of *who,* is also used for either people or things by many writers, although a few purists object:

Lyly is a playwright **whose plays are seldom put on.**

The Bugle is a paper **whose editorial policies I detest.**

(The alternative to *whose* for nonhuman nominals—*of which*—is sometimes stiffly formal or cumbersome: The Bugle *is a paper the editorial policies of which I detest.*)

125

You can make an adjectival clause out of almost any sentence that helps to identify the person or thing a nominal refers to. Take these sentences for example:

A. The robbers held up the cafeteria.
B. The robbers wore Halloween masks.

Sentence A can be embedded in Sentence B in two steps:

1. Insert Sentence A in B right after the nominal it is going to modify:

The robbers (the robbers held up the cafeteria) wore Halloween masks.

2. Substitute the includer *who* (or *that*) for the subject of the included clause:

who

The robbers (the robbers held up the cafeteria) wore Halloween masks.

The result:

The robbers **who held up the cafeteria** wore Halloween masks.

If the subject of the sentence to be embedded is not the same as the nominal the clause will modify, an extra step is necessary. Take these sentences:

A. I recommended the man.
B. The boss hired the man.

1. The embedded clause will modify the nominal *the man,* so we will insert it after that nominal:

The boss hired the man (I recommended the man).

2. Next, we must move the nominal in A that duplicates the one to be modified up to the front of the embedded sentence:

The boss hired the man (the man I recommended).

3. Now we can substitute *that* for the nominal in B to make it an included clause:

that

The boss hired the man (the man I recommended).

The result:

The boss hired the man **that I recommended.**

Note: The includer *whom* could be used instead of *that* in the example above, or the includer could be omitted altogether:

The boss hired the man whom I recommended.
The boss hired the man I recommended.

The last way is not always possible. For instance, you cannot use it if the includer replaces the subject of the embedded sentence. For instance, you cannot omit the *that* in the sentence you worked through earlier:

The robbers who held up the cafeteria wore Halloween masks.
*The robbers held up the cafeteria wore Halloween masks.

As for *whom,* it is a good idea to avoid it whenever possible. If you do use it, you run the risk of putting it in where *who* belongs. (More often than not, *who* is the right choice.)

PRACTICE 3

Combine each pair of sentences by embedding the first in the second as an adjectival clause. If the subject of the first sentence is the same as the nominal to be modified, use the two steps shown in Section 12.3. If the subject of the first sentence is different from the nominal to be modified, use the three steps shown in the example.

Example: You would like this book.
This is a book.

1. This is a book (you would like this book).
2. This is a book (this book you would like).
               that
3. This is a book (~~this book~~ you would like).

1. The man needs no introduction.
I am about to introduce a man.

_____

_____

_____

2. The people live in glass houses.
   The people should not throw stones.

   _____

   _____

   _____

3. The person threw the egg at the speaker.
   Will the person please raise his hand?

   _____

   _____

   _____

4. Susan served the cheese at her party.
   The cheese was delicious.

   _____

   _____

   _____

TASK A

Rewrite the subject nominal of each sentence in the space provided and place cluster marks before and after it. Then put an asterisk under the nucleus and mark each modifier with an arrow beneath it. Use one unbroken arrow to mark the prepositional phrase.

Example: The students of Oxford used to make their own ale.

Ʞ the students of Oxford Ʞ
→   *   ←

1. A malt liquor known as *ale* is the national drink of England.

2. The Anglo-Saxon word for the original ale was *bere.*

3. The English ale of the fifteenth century was different from ale today.

4. The people of ancient Egypt used beer medicinally.

5. This strong drink of the Egyptians was called *barley-wine* or *hemki*.

TASK B

The information given in the following pairs of sentences can be compressed into one. There are two ways to do this: (1) by using a predicatid and (2) by using an included clause. Use each method in the appropriate blank.

Example: The man is drinking beer.
            The man is Harry.

(*predicatid*)   The man drinking beer is Harry.
(*clause*)   The man who is drinking beer is Harry.

1. The bird is hovering overhead.
   The bird is a vulture.

(predicatid) _____

(clause) _____

2. The book was written in 1901.
   The book is on the origins of beer and ale.
   (Note that the verb in this predicatid does not end in *-ing*.)

(predicatid) _____

(clause) _____

3. The detective was looking for clues.
   The detective had a puzzled expression on his face.

(predicatid) _____

(clause) _____

4. The horse was carrying a fat jockey.
   The horse got tired.

(predicatid) _____

(clause) _____

5. The man was smoking a trick cigar.
   The man could not imagine what was so funny.

(predicatid) _____

(clause) _____

TASK C

Read the following paragraphs. Adjectival modifiers have been under-lined. Mark each one as follows:

1. If the modifier is a phrase, put the marks < > around it.
2. If it is a predicatid, use the marks ∤   ∤.
3. If it is an included clause, put brackets [   ] around it.

Place an asterisk under the nucleus of the noun cluster—that is, the noun the adjectival modifier modifies.

Every adult <u>living in this country</u> has probably tasted beer <u>of some kind</u>. But on the subject <u>of brewing</u>, most people have ideas <u>that are quite vague</u>. Contrary to the idea <u>held by most adults</u>, pale ale does not consist solely of hops and water; the malt <u>which the brewer uses</u> is an essential ingredient <u>of both beer and ale</u>.

Old ballad makers have sung its praises, but few prose writers have touched upon the subject <u>of beer</u>, and <u>those who have written about it</u> have done so only in a superficial manner.

TASK D

Write a paragraph about your favorite food or drink. Try to vary your noun clusters by including phrases, predicatids, and clauses among the adjectival modifiers in the clusters.

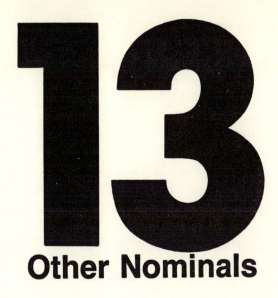

Other Nominals

13.1 Nominal Clauses

The most common kinds of nominals, of course, are noun clusters and pro-nominals—but clauses and predicatids can also be used as nominals.

In Unit 8, we examined adverbial clauses—included clauses used in adverbial positions (such as the F and E positions). We saw that adverbial clauses are commonly introduced by a special subset of includers, such as *after, because, since, when, if,* and *although,* which are called **adverbial includers.**

In Unit 12, we examined adjectival clauses—included clauses used in adjectival positions following nouns inside noun clusters. We saw that adjectival clauses are commonly introduced by another special subset of the includers—that is, by includers like *that* and WH words (*which, who, whom, whose, where,* and *when*)—which are called **adjectival includers** when they introduce adjectival clauses.

There is still another kind of clause. **Nominal clauses** are included clauses used in nominal positions (such as the S, Y, O, and pO positions). Nominal clauses are commonly introduced by still a third subset of the includers; namely, includers like *that, if, whether, what, how,* and the WH words, all of which are called **nominal includers** when they are used to introduce nominal clauses.

One of the most common uses of nominal clauses is as objects in the O position following verbs like *say, think, believe, know, hear, ask,* and *wonder.* Note that we can easily change most sentences into nominal clauses by merely adding nominal includers to them. Look at the example at the top of the next page.

Statement: Sam often walks in the park alone at night.
Nominal clause: [that Sam often walks in the park alone at night]

O

Clause as object: I have heard [that Sam often walks in the park alone at night].

The includer *that* can usually be omitted from a nominal clause in the O position, just as *that* can be omitted from an adjectival clause.

O

Clause as object: They say [that Sam often walks in the park alone at night].

or: They say [Sam often walks in the park alone at night].

A nominal clause introduced by *that* is sometimes used to fill the S position:

S   P
[That Sam often walks in the park alone at night]] is surprising.

S   P
or: [That Sam should go walking alone]] surprises me.

You will notice, however, that sentences like these have long subjects followed by short predicates. This is contrary to the tendency in present-day English, which is to pile up new information toward the end of the sentence. In order to avoid long subjects like those in the last two examples, we often replace the subject clause in the S position with the **filler** *it* and postpone the subject to a position at the end of the sentence (which we will call "the PP position": *PP* stands for "postponed"). Only nominal clauses introduced by *that* can be postponed in this way, but it is a very common practice to begin a sentence with the subject filler *it,* postponing the real subject (the subject clause) to the end of the sentence. For example:

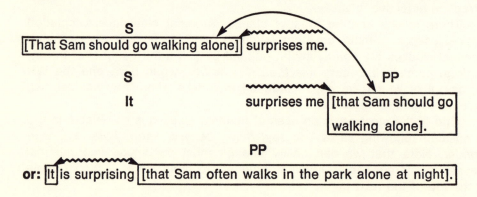

Nominal clauses commonly fill the O position, the S position, the PP position, and—less commonly—a pO position. In some sentences you will even find two nominal clauses filling two different positions. For example:

```
       S              X                    Y
[What surprises me] is [[that Sam should go walking in the park alone]].
```

```
       S                   X     V         O
[Whoever stole my wallet] has discovered [that it was empty].
```

PRACTICE 1

Each sentence below contains one or more nominal clauses. Draw a box around each nominal clause and mark it *S*, *O*, *Y*, or *PP*, depending on its position in the sentence. Draw square brackets around the clauses inside the boxes. (The first one has been done for you.)

```
                                PP
1. It is true [[that sports records are made to be broken]].
```

2. No one doubted that Henry Aaron would break Babe Ruth's home run record.

3. But what no one knew was just when he would break the record.

4. Even now it seems quite amazing that he did it during the Braves' first home game right after special ceremonies in his honor.

5. How soon somebody else will break Aaron's record is anyone's guess.

6. Many sports writers don't think it will happen in the near future.

7. In fact, some doubt whether the new record will ever be broken.

8. But it may be possible that some Little Leaguer of today will be the Henry Aaron of tomorrow.

13.2 Nominal Predicatids

We can also use predicatids in nominal positions. For example:

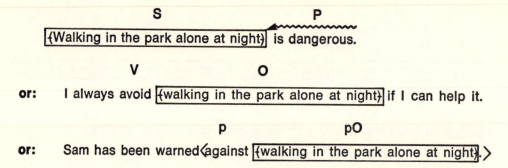

The predicatid in each of the last three examples is an **ING predicatid** —that is, a predicatid introduced by the ING form of a verb. We can also use a **TO predicatid**—that is, a predicatid introduced by the word *to* followed by the base form of some verb (e.g., *to walk)*—in *some* nominal positions. For example:

S   P
{To walk in the park alone at night} is dangerous.

We can replace a TO predicatid in the S position with the filler *it* and then postpone the predicatid to the PP position, just as we can a *that* clause in the S position. For example:

S   PP
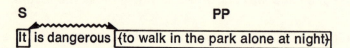
It is dangerous {to walk in the park alone at night}

We can use ING predicatids after possessives or after possessive determiners, to form "predicatid clusters." For example:

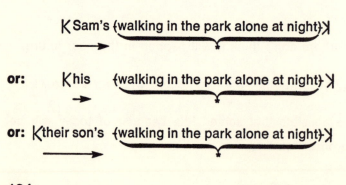

We can use predicatid clusters like these in most nominal positions. For example:

S   P
| Sam's walking in the park alone at night | worries his parents.

V   O
They do not like | his walking in the park alone at night. |

p   pO
They are concerned < about | their son's walking in the park

alone at night | >.

X   Y
The cause of their concern is | Sam's walking in the park alone at night. |

PRACTICE 2

Fill in each blank below with a *nominal predicatid* of your own choosing and then mark the position that it fills in its sentence. You will have to use either an ING predicatid or a TO predicatid in each case. (The first sentence has been done for you.)

O
1. Sandy loves to travel every year on her vacation. _____

2. John's favorite hobby is _____

3. _____ can be fun.

4. It is only human _____

5. Are you worried about _____?

6. _____ should interest you.

7. What I want most is _____

8. _____ makes me angry.

9. I discovered _____.

10. It is unfortunate _____.

TASK A

Find the nominal clause or predicatid in each of the following sentences and draw a box around it. Indicate, by writing *S, Y, O,* or *PP* above each box, whether the nominal is in the subject, object, predicator, or postponed position in the sentence. Then bring the nominal down to the next line and mark it with crossed parentheses (⧼ ⧽) if it is a predicatid, or with square brackets ([]) if it is a clause. (The first sentence has been done for you.)

1. In 1871, at the age of 41, the German archeologist Heinrich Schlie-

    O

    mann began ⎡proving the reality of Homer's *Iliad* and *Odyssey*.⎤

    ⧼proving the reality of Homer's Iliad and Odyssey⧽

2. One of Schliemann's fondest dreams was to find the ancient city of Troy.

3. He believed that Homer's Troy was buried under the Turkish city of Hissarlik.

4. But many German scholars and archeologists insisted that another Turkish city was the correct location.

5. Digging under Hissarlik was indeed the right course of action.

6. It took Schliemann many years to find Homer's cities.

7. Traveling through Greece, Crete, and Turkey fulfilled his long-held childhood ambition.

8. As a child, he had wondered why Homer's tales were considered purely fictional by historians.

TASK B

Each of the following sentences contains a clause or TO predicatid in the S position. Underline the clause or predicatid, and then rewrite the sentence, replacing the subject with *it* and moving the clause or predicatid to the PP position at the end. Follow the example.

Example: That Schliemann recorded his findings in books he wrote while in Greece is fortunate.

It is fortunate that Schliemann recorded his findings in books he wrote while in Greece.

1. That English scholars and archeologists recognized the importance of Schliemann's work is a credit to their foresight.

_____

_____

2. To prove the reality of Homer's epics about Troy was the goal of Schliemann's life's work.

_____

_____

3. That German scholars refused to accept the validity of his work was a testimony to their narrow-mindedness.

_____

_____

4. To fall in love with a beautiful young Greek girl was only natural for a romantic like Schliemann.

_____

_____

5. That he was a romantic is hardly disputable.

_____

6. That Schliemann never lost his enthusiasm is fortunate.

_____

_____

TASK C

The following paragraphs contain four different kinds of nominals used as subjects. Find each subject and show what kind of nominal it is by marking it in this way: If the subject consists of a noun cluster or a single noun, place the marks Ϟ Ϡ before and after it, mark the nucleus with an asterisk, and draw arrows under any modifiers pointing toward the asterisk; if the subject consists only of a pro-nominal, draw a box around it; if the subject consists of a clause, place square brackets ([]) before and after it; if the subject is a predicatid, place the marks ﴾ ﴿ before and after it. (The first subject has been marked for you.)

Ϟ German scholars of the late nineteenth century Ϡ believed that Homer's Troy was buried under the Turkish city of Bounarbashi. They refused even to consider the opinion of Heinrich Schliemann, because Schliemann had not been educated at a university. He was a businessman who had taken up archeology as an avocation. But, as you know, a person's hobby often develops into the main interest in his life.

Schliemann believed, as a result of his reading of Homer's *Iliad* and *Odyssey,* that Troy was buried under Hissarlik, another city in Turkey. Accumulating enough money to pursue his archeological interests took Schliemann about twenty years. To dig under Hissarlik turned out to be the right course of action. That Hissarlik was indeed the site of the ancient city of Troy was eventually proven beyond any doubt.

At first the German scholars of his day refused even to listen to Schliemann's views. To recognize the full significance of his work took them a long time. But even from the first, British scholars and archeologists recognized its importance and encouraged him in his research.

TASK D

Write three paragraphs (about fifteen to twenty sentences in all), telling about a childhood ambition that you have hopes of fulfilling some day. Try to vary your nominals by using clauses and predicatids, as well as noun clusters and pro-nominals.

Time-
Relationship
in Clauses

14.1 Past and Present

Every English sentence is time-oriented; that is, its content is always related to some definite time in the past, or else to the present—to "now."
The specific time-orientation of a sentence is signaled by the form of the
main verb—that is, the verb in the trunk. For instance, the first of the following sentences is tied to some past time, the second to the present. In
both these examples, the form of the main verb in boldface type establishes
the tie:

> *Past:*   Last week he **said** that he liked cornflakes.
> *Present:*   He still **says** that he likes cornflakes.

The tie with a specific time in the past is designated by the **past** form of a
verb, the form that most often ends in *-d, -ed,* or *-t* (e.g. *lived, wanted,
spent*). The tie with the present is signaled by the **present** form, the form
with an *-s* or *-es* ending, or with no ending at all, depending upon the subject (e.g., *he lives, she goes, they go*).

PRACTICE 1

Each of the following sentences contains a present or past verb form,
which is underlined. In the space below each sentence write a different
sentence, using the same verb but changing its time-orientation. Indicate

the time-orientation of each sentence by writing *past* or *present* after the sentence. Follow the example.

Example: Yesterday morning Mr. Muller <u>jogged</u> for a mile.   (past)

Mr. Muller <u>jogs</u> for a mile every day.   (present)

1. Last night Albert <u>decided</u> to call Grace.

_____

2. Grace always <u>looks</u> like a million.

_____

3. My little sister still <u>believes</u> in Santa Claus.

_____

4. Last year the Lasalles <u>went</u> to Alaska on their vacation.

_____

14.2   The Three Kinds of Time-Relationship

Once the general time-orientation of a sentence—past or present—has been established, there are three kinds of **time-relationships** that can be expressed in included clauses: **earlier time, same time,** and **later time.** In speaking of two past events, we can say that A happened before B, at the same time as B, or later than B. In speaking of the present, we can say that A has already happened and that B is happening now, that A and B are both happening now, or that A is happening now and that B will happen at some time in the future. All three time-relationships are possible when speaking of either the past or the present. The reference point is established by the main verb, and the specific time-relationships are then expressed by X-words in the included clauses.

The following example shows a sentence that has *past* orientation:

Last Tuesday morning, Dr. Day <u>phoned</u> the office. He <u>said</u> that his car <u>had</u> broken down and that it <u>would</u> be at least another hour before he <u>could</u> get there.

Notice that all of the underlined verbs or X-words relate to a specific moment in the past—the moment last Tuesday morning when Dr. Day telephoned. As a result, all of the verbs and X-words appear in their past-tense forms. But in addition, all of the X-words in the included clauses—*had* (*broken down*), *would* (*be*), and *could* (*get there*)—also show *time-relation-*

ship to the time of the main verbs (*phoned* and *said*). The specific relationships are the following:

Earlier time: had (*broken down*)[1]
Later time: would (*be*), could (*get there*)

Time-relationships can also be shown with respect to present time. Suppose that Dr. Day is on the phone right now and that his nurse is reporting what he is saying. She might say:

Dr. Day <u>says</u> that his car <u>has</u> broken down and that it <u>will</u> be at least another hour before he <u>can</u> get here.

In this sentence the included clause *that his car has broken down* refers to something that happened *before* Dr. Day's phoning (that is, at an *earlier time* than *now*), and the included clause *that it will be at least another hour before he can get here* refers to something that Dr. Day anticipates as likely to happen *after* his phoning (that is, at a *later time*). The relationships for present time are the following:

Earlier time: has (*broken down*)
Later time: will (*be*)

All three kinds of time-relationship can be shown graphically in a "Time Chart" like this one:

TIME CHART

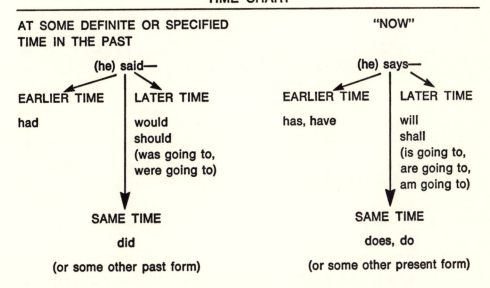

AT SOME DEFINITE OR SPECIFIED TIME IN THE PAST   "NOW"

(he) said—

EARLIER TIME	LATER TIME
had	would
	should
	(was going to,
	were going to)

SAME TIME

did

(or some other past form)

(he) says—

EARLIER TIME	LATER TIME
has, have	will
	shall
	(is going to,
	are going to,
	am going to)

SAME TIME

does, do

(or some other present form)

---

[1] The form of the verb used after *had, have,* or *has* is called the **D-T-N form**, since it usually ends in *-d, -t,* or *-n* (e.g. *had lived, had slept, had eaten*). All regular D-T-N forms end in *-d* or *-ed,* just like regular past forms, but English also has many irregular D-T-N forms (like *slept* and *eaten*). You will find several irregular D-T-N forms listed on pages 164-65.

PRACTICE 2

Change the time-orientation of each of the sentences below. This will mean that you will have to change the verb in the trunk and also all the X-words or verbs in the included clauses. Do not change the *time-relationship* between the main verb or verbs and the others. Use the Time Chart on page 141 if you want to. (The first sentence has been done for you.)

1. Mischa <u>thinks</u> that he <u>will</u> try clams again and that maybe he <u>will</u> even taste mussels.
   Mischa <u>thought</u> that he <u>would</u> try clams again and that maybe he

   <u>would</u> even taste mussels.

2. Grace <u>told</u> Albert that she <u>would</u> go to the dance with him if he <u>would</u> grow a mustache.

   _____

   _____

3. Albert <u>insists</u> that he <u>is going to</u> grow the most handsome mustache in town.

   _____

   _____

4. Mr. Muller <u>guesses</u> that he <u>has</u> traveled the distance from New York to Chicago since he <u>has</u> been jogging.

   _____

   _____

5. He <u>thinks</u> that he <u>will</u> surely jog the distance from Chicago to San Francisco by the end of the year.

   _____

   _____

6. My little brother <u>didn't</u> believe me when I <u>told</u> him that there <u>was</u> no Easter bunny.

   _____

   _____

7. The Lasalles always <u>take</u> a trip after the children <u>have</u> finished school; they <u>will</u> return in time for the new year.

_____

_____

8. Marie <u>buys</u> a whole new wardrobe whenever the styles <u>change</u> and she <u>feels</u> that her clothes <u>have</u> become unfashionable.

_____

_____

14.3 More About Time-Relationship

It is important to remember that the forms listed in the left half of the Time Chart on page 141 show earlier time, same time, and later time not only with reference to the time of (*he*) *said*—but also with reference to all past forms in their own sentences. Suppose, for example, that we want to express all of the following ideas in one sentence:

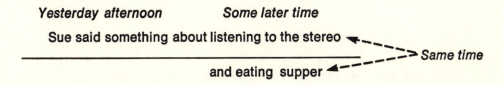

Yesterday afternoon   *Some later time*

Sue said something about listening to the stereo

and eating supper   *Same time*

We could show the different time-relationships holding between the various events by using time-relationship X-words, as in the following sentence:

Yesterday afternoon Sue *said* that she *would listen* to the stereo while she *ate* supper.

The X-word *would* in the included *that* clause shows that Sue expected her listening to the stereo to take place at a "later time" than the time of her speaking; the past verb *ate* in the *while* clause (which is embedded in the *that* clause) shows that Sue expected to eat supper at the "same time" as the time of her listening to the stereo.
But suppose, instead, that we want to express these ideas:

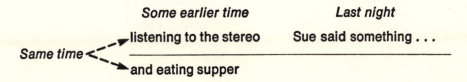

Some earlier time   *Last night*

listening to the stereo   Sue said something . . .

Same time

and eating supper

We would now show the time-relationships holding between the various events in the following way:

> Last night Sue *said* that she *had listened* to the stereo while she *ate* supper.

Here the X-word *had* shows that Sue's listening to the stereo took place at an "earlier time" than her speaking about it. The past form *ate* appears in a clause that is embedded in the larger clause *that she had listened to the stereo while she ate supper* and shows that Sue ate supper at the "same time" that she listened to the stereo. In other words, the included *while* clause expresses the same time-relationship to the main verb (*said*) as that of the clause in which it is included. (That is, since her eating supper took place at the same time as her listening to the stereo, both of those events must have taken place *before* she *said* anything.)

Much the same is true of events described in a sentence that has present time-orientation. Suppose that we want to express these ideas:

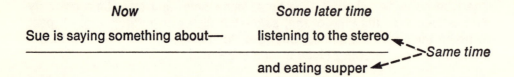

We can show the various time-relationships in the following way:

> Sue *says* that she *will listen* to the stereo while she *eats* supper.

In this sentence, the verb *eats* appears in the clause *while she eats supper,* which is embedded in the larger clause *that she will listen to the stereo while she eats supper.* As before, the time-relationship of the larger clause carries over to the clause included in it. Thus we understand the sentence to mean that Sue will eat supper at the "same time" that she listens to the stereo (which will be at a "later time" than "now").

PRACTICE 3

In each space that follows, write a sentence that shows the time-relationship described above it. (The first sentence has been done for you.)

1. *Last evening*   *Some later time*
   I said—   calling you

   Last evening I said that I would call you.

2. *Yesterday*   *Some later time*
   Don decided   studying for the test
                                                    ⟍ *Same time*
                                and eating lunch

_____

_____

3.   *Earlier time*   *Last week*
                going to Europe   Aunt Edith told me
   same time
                and being twenty-
                one years old

_____

_____

4. *Now*   *Some later time*
   Mrs. Vaughn is saying we—   giving the recital
                                                    ⟍ *Same time*
                                  and being ready

_____

_____

5.   *Earlier time*   *This morning*
                eating all the cookies   My little brother said . . .
   same time
                and Mother being out

_____

_____

6. *Now*   *Some later time*
   Tom's uncle says that Tom—   inheriting the money
                                                    ⟍ *Same time*
                                  and getting married

_____

_____

14.4 Overlapping

There is one other kind of time-relationship, a time-relationship which—for lack of a better name—we will call overlapping time-relationship. The signals for overlapping time-relationship are the forms of *to be: was, were, is, are, am, be, been,* and *being.* For example, if we want to express some activity or state of affairs that overlapped the time of Dr. Day's telephone call last Tuesday morning—something that was going on before his call and that probably continued even after his call—we can do so by using the X-word *was* or *were* with the ING form of some verb, instead of using the past form of the verb. In other words, instead of saying **When Dr. Day phoned, several persons waited in his office,* we would say *When Dr. Day phoned, several persons were waiting in his office.* Or again, if we want to show some activity or state of affairs overlapping this moment, "now," we can do so by using the X-word *am* or *are* or *is* with the ING form of the verb: *I am still waiting in his office now.*[1]

We can show this overlapping kind of time-relationship this way:

AT SOME DEFINITE OR SPECIFIED   "NOW"
TIME IN THE PAST

several persons were waiting in   I am still waiting in his
his office   office

These are probably the two most common kinds of overlapping. There are, however, several others. It is possible, for example, to show that an activity or state of affairs began before some moment in the past and continued up to and perhaps even overlapped that moment (or has continued up to and will overlap this moment, "now"); it is also possible to show that an activity or state of affairs started at or just before some moment in the past and continued on, perhaps indefinitely, after that moment (or that it has just started and will continue on, perhaps indefinitely, into the future). To show these special kinds of overlapping, we add *been* or *be* to either the "earlier time-relationship" X-words or to the "later time-relationship" X-words. For example:

> When Dr. Day finally *arrived*, several people *had been waiting* for hours.

> When Dr. Day *comes* in, I *will* still *be waiting.*

---

[1] ING forms are listed under *was, were, is, are, am, be, been,* and *being,* in the Verb Key on page 164; the Verb Key shows that ING forms are the forms that regularly follow X-words like *was, were, is,* and the like, just as base forms are the forms that regularly follow *would, will, can, must, did, doesn't, don't,* and the predicatid signal *to* as in *to walk.*

146

Here is the Time Chart again, with the forms showing overlapping time-relationships added, in heavy black type:

TIME CHART

AT SOME DEFINITE OR SPECIFIED TIME IN THE PAST		"NOW"	
EARLIER TIME	LATER TIME	EARLIER TIME	LATER TIME
had	would	have, has	will
had been	**would be**	**have been,**	**will be**
		has been	

SAME TIME

did
(or some other past form)[1]
were, was

SAME TIME

does, do
(or some other present form)
is, are, am

PRACTICE 4

Write the appropriate time-relationship signals in the blank spaces in each sentence below. Note that most of these signals—but not all of them—are X-words. As you fill in the blanks, look at the Time Chart just above, and see if you can find the forms that you are using in the Chart. Note that all of the forms have curved arrows under them in the Chart to suggest "overlapping." (The first sentence has been done for you.)

1. When I phoned the theater a month ago, the manager told me that they ____were____ showing the film ____*Hex.*____

2. That was the same film that they _____ _____ showing since the beginning of the preceding month.

3. It was such a popular film that the manager thought they _____ probably _____ showing it for the next three or four weeks.

4. According to the newspaper, they _____ still showing the film there this week.

---

[1] A series of past forms are often used one after the other to show that a series of events took place in succession, almost as if they were happening "at the same time." For example, "Roy *jumped* out of bed, *looked* at his clock, *dressed* in a great hurry, and *dashed* out of the house."

5. That means that they _____ already _____ showing *Hex* at that theatre for at least two months.

6. If it continues to attract large crowds, they _____ probably

_____ showing it for still another two or three weeks.

TASK A

Assume that the sentences appearing below are part of a conversation between two students—a conversation that is taking place *late in February*. The students are talking about books that have been assigned as outside reading in one student's literature class *this* term, as well as about books that were assigned *last* term. Fill in all the blanks with the proper X-words and verb forms *or both,* in order to show the *time-relationship* of each event *to the time of the conversation,* or *to some time in the past mentioned by one of the students.* (The verb to be used in each sentence is shown in parentheses at the end of the sentence. The first sentence has been done for you.)
Note: If you are ever in doubt as to what form of a given verb to use after a specific X-word, consult the Verb Key on pages 164-65. If you are ever in doubt as to what X-word to use for a specific time-relationship, consult the Time Chart on page 147.

First Student: How many books _____ Professor

Hunt _____ for outside reading this term? (Use the verb *assign.*)

Second Student: He _____ seven. (Use the verb *assign* again.)

First Student: Seven! How _____ any one _____ seven books in one term? (Use *read.*)

Second Student: Hunt _____ us to read one book every two weeks. (Use *expect.*)

First Student: How many of the seven _____ you

already _____? (Use *read.*)

Second Student: I _____n't _____ any of

them yet. (Use *read.*) I _____ too much other work to do for my other courses. (Use *have.*)

First Student: Then what _____ you _____?

(Use *do*.) How _____ you _____ ready for the final exam in May? (Use *get*.)

Second Student: Oh, I _____ _____ all the books

during the spring vacation, while I _____ at

my grandparents'. (Use *read*.) There _____n't

anything else to do there. There never _____. (Use forms of *to be* in both of these last sentences.)

First Student: _____ you already _____ all the books? (Use *buy*.)

Second Student: No, I _____ _____ only
1
four of them. (Use *buy* again.) I _____
1
_____ the rest next week, after I
2   2
_____ _____ studying
3
for the history quiz that we _____ prob-
3
ably _____ on Monday. (Use the verbs

buy (1), *finish* (2), and *have* (3).) I _____ too busy now. (Use some form of *to be*.)

First Student: _____ Hunt _____ the same number of books last term? (Use *assign*.)

Second Student: Yes, he _____.

First Student: I suppose you _____ all of *them* at the same time too—during vacation? (Use *read*.)

Second Student: No. I knew that I _____n't _____

any time to read while I _____ at home for Christmas. (Use *have* and then some form of

to be.) So I _____ one book every two

weeks. (Use *read*.)

TASK B

Mrs. Mackenzie lives in Nearfield and regularly does her grocery shopping at Dolly's Deli. Yesterday afternoon she phoned the delicatessen to place an order for sugar. In the first paragraph below you will find a report of her phone call. Assume that, instead of phoning yesterday, *she has just finished calling* and that you are the clerk who took the call and are now reporting it to the owner of the delicatessen. Begin your paragraph with the words "It's Mrs. MacKenzie. She says that she has seen the advertisement—" Choose your X-words and verb forms carefully.

Mrs. Mackenzie called Dolly's Deli yesterday afternoon to say that she had seen the advertisement for the special sale on sugar in the *Daily Blurb* and wondered if the sale was still on. She was completely out of sugar, since she had just finished making several jars of apple jelly. She needed some sugar right away for a pie she was about to bake, and she would need quite a bit of sugar the next morning since she also wanted to make some grape jelly. She said that if the sale was still on, she would phone her husband and ask him to pick up two five-pound bags when he drove past on his way home from his office.

_____

_____

_____

_____

_____

_____

_____

_____

_____

_____

_____

_____

_____

TASK C

In the following passage, the narrator is speaking about a severe snow storm which had caused a large truck to block a mountain pass. Underline each of the X-words (or X-word + verb form combinations) which express the time-relationship. Indicate above them whether they show *earlier time* (ET), *same time* (ST), or *later time* (LT). Remember that past verb forms also show time-relationships: They show that some event occurred at the *same time* as (or just a moment later than) some other event. (The first sentences have been done for you.)

(ST)

At the actual block the situation <u>was</u> better. The left-hand lane on the

(ET)

upper side <u>had been cleared.</u> Then the truck drivers had got together . . .

to help the truck that was in trouble. They had brought forward another truck

and [had] got a chain from it to the one which was slewed across the road.

There was not much room to maneuver, and the darkness and flying snow

impeded the work and slowed it down. Still, they were moving the stalled

truck a foot at a time, and would have it out of the jam and back on the road

in a few minutes. Working with the truck drivers and really directing the show

was the man with the city overcoat who had volunteered to help; but he was

so covered with snow that now you couldn't [tell] what he was wearing.

The Superintendent took charge, but there was nothing much more for

him to do. Thank God for truck drivers! It's the professionals that keep going

in time of trouble. But the man in the city overcoat and the others who had

come to help were all right too.

—from *Storm* by George R. Stewart

TASK D

Write five to ten sentences describing a dream or dreams you used to have when you were younger—dreams about things that you would do when you got older. Then write five other sentences describing your *present* plans for the future. Be sure to use the appropriate X-words and verb forms to show the different time-relationships involved.

Adding
Something Extra

15.1 Inserts

A writer may add an insert to provide additional information—information that is not really essential to what he is saying in the rest of the sentence. In such cases he will usually "set off" or "cut off" the insert from the rest of the sentence by means of punctuation marks. This is especially true when the insert interrupts the flow of the rest of the sentence. For example:

> Early printers inserted a *g* in the word *sovereign* **(Chaucer spelled it sovereyn)** in the mistaken notion that this word was related to the verb *reign*.

When the insert itself is fairly long or when what it says is only loosely related to the rest of the sentence, it is often set off from the units before and after it by means of parentheses, as in the example above.

Commas are often used instead of parentheses, especially if the insert itself is fairly short or if the information that it conveys is related to the ideas expressed by the rest of the sentence. For example:

> The most important signal in present-day English, **needless to say,** is the order of the positions for different units.

> King Alfred's English, **unlike our own,** had a fairly flexible word order.

Some writers occasionally use dashes instead of commas before and after an insert, especially when there already are other commas in a sentence. Many writers, however, avoid all use of dashes in their edited English. But by alternating between the use of commas and dashes and the use of parentheses, a writer can often suggest different degrees of tightness **or looseness** in the relationship of inserts within other inserts. For example:

In the English of King Alfred's day **(or, as it is commonly called, *Old English*),** the subject nominals were distinguished from the object nominals by their endings. As a result, the ordering of positions in Old English sentences, **unlike the relatively fixed order found in Modern English,** was rather flexible—**so flexible, in fact, that in many sentences the subject followed the verb.**

PRACTICE 1

The items labeled *insert* below can be added to the sentences that follow. Rewrite each sentence with the insert included. Use either parentheses or commas to set off the insert, whichever seems better. (The first one has been done for you.)

1. Insert: unfortunately
   Sentence: The words that Chaucer spelled *dette* and *doute* were respelled as *debt* and *doubt* to suggest a relationship with Latin words.

   The words that Chaucer spelled *dette* and *doute* were, unfortunately,

   respelled as *debt* and *doubt* to suggest a relationship with Latin words.

2. Insert: similar but not directly related to the porcupine
   Sentence: The hedgehog is famous for having one big idea about how to defend himself.

   _____

   _____

3. Insert: whatever the threat
   Sentence: The hedgehog always rolls up into a prickly ball.

   _____

   _____

4. Insert: On the other hand
   Sentence: The fox has a variety of different defense plans to choose from.

   _____

   _____

5. Insert: by way of illustration
   Sentence: The philosopher Isaiah Berlin uses these two animals
               to characterize two opposite kinds of human minds.

_____

_____

6. Insert: at least I have always thought of myself that way
   Sentence: I am wily like the fox.

_____

_____

15.2 Appositives and Nonrestrictive Clauses

There are two kinds of inserts that are so common in present-day English that they are given special labels in many grammar books. Both kinds are always inserted after nominals; both kinds are used for giving additional information about the nominals—that is, both kinds make additional predications about the nominals that they follow. They are usually (but not always) separated from their nominals and from the rest of their sentences by means of commas.

The first of these two kinds of inserts consists of a noun cluster. In many grammar books such inserts are called **appositives;** they are said to be **in apposition with** the nominals that precede them. For example:

There were differences between ⎡Old English⎤, ⟨the English of King

Alfred's day,⟩ and ⎡Middle English⎤, ⟨the English of Chaucer's time.⟩

Note that it is usually possible to form a perfectly natural sentence by using the preceding nominal as the subject before *were, was, are,* or *is,* followed by the appositive used as a predicator in the Y position. For example:

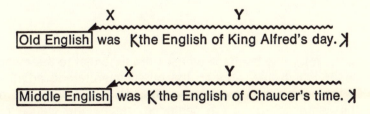

155

The second kind of insert consists of a clause introduced by a WH word. This insert, called a **nonrestrictive clause,** looks exactly like an adjectival clause. The only difference is that the nonrestrictive clause gives additional but nonessential information about the nominal it follows. In other words, the information given in a nonrestrictive clause is not strictly necessary for understanding what the nominal refers to. These examples should help to make the difference clear:

The American river **that flows north** is the Red River. (adjectival clause)

The Mississippi River, **which once flowed north into Hudson's Bay,** flows south into the Gulf of Mexico. (nonrestrictive clause)

In sentence A, the boldface clause is essential because it identifies the American river that flows north. In Sentence B, the boldface clause gives interesting but nonessential information. The sentence makes sense without the clause:

The Mississippi River flows south into the Gulf of Mexico.

The main reason for knowing about nonrestrictive clauses is that it is customary to set them off with commas—unlike adjectival clauses, which are not set off. The following example contains two nonrestrictive clauses:

There are many differences between Old English, **which was spoken in King Alfred's day,** and Middle English, **which was spoken in Chaucer's time.**

As you can see, the sentence still makes sense with the nonrestrictive clauses dropped out:

There were many differences between Old English and Middle English.

If you have trouble deciding whether a clause should be set off with commas, try reading the sentence without the clause. If it makes sense that way, set the clause off with commas. If the sentence doesn't make sense without the clause, don't set it off.

PRACTICE 2

Some of the following boldface clauses are essential to the meaning of the sentences in which they appear; the others merely add additional information. If the clause is nonrestrictive—that is, if the clause is not essential to the sentence—copy the sentence, setting the clause off with commas. If the clause cannot be dropped out, simply write a *C* to show that the sentence is correctly punctuated. (The first one has been done for you.)

1. Anton van Leeuwenhoek **who was a Dutch naturalist** invented the microscope.

   Anton van Leeuwenhoek, who was a Dutch naturalist, invented the

   microscope.

2. People **who live in glass houses** should not throw stones.

   _____

   _____

3. King Roderick **who had no sense of humor** had trouble hiring a court jester.

   _____

   _____

4. The movie **that I wanted to see** is no longer on.

   _____

   _____

5. Nancy Brady **who was favored to win the tournament** drew a bye in the first round.

   _____

   _____

6. Murchison's new play **which most of the critics did not like** was a smashing success at the box office.

   _____

   _____

7. Each person **who enters the contest** must send in two box tops.

   _____

15.3 Loading Sentences

Throughout this book, you have been working with the constructions that characterize mature written English. Most of them provide a way of pulling together loosely related ideas into clear and effective written statements. The tasks that follow will give you a chance to review some of the major methods of combining sentences and expanding nominals. Section numbers have been provided in the event you feel the need to review certain constructions.

TASK A

Combine the following pairs of sentences according to the bracketed instructions.

1. Wellington encountered Napoleon at Waterloo.
   Wellington defeated him decisively.
   [Use a coordinator to form a compound predicate. (§ 7.2)]

   _____

   _____

2. [Make a half-sentence out of the second sentence in 1 above and add it after *Waterloo*. (§ 9.3)]

   _____

   _____

3. [This time, make the second sentence in 1 into a nonrestrictive clause following *Waterloo*. Use *where* as your includer. Your sentence will sound better if you use the pro-nominal *he* in the nonrestrictive clause. (§ 12.3)]

   _____

   _____

4. Napoleon chose to fight the battle in Belgium.
   He wanted to prevent an invasion of France.
   [Make the second sentence into an included clause and embed it in the *E* position of the first sentence. (§ 8.1)]

   _____

   _____

5. Napoleon was confident of victory.
He had his Imperial Guard carry their dress uniforms in their packs.
[Make the first sentence into an included clause and embed it in the *F* position in the second sentence. (§ 8.1)]

_____

_____

_____

6. He thought they would need them.
They made their triumphant entry into Brussels.
[Make the second sentence into an included clause and embed it in the *E* position of the first sentence. Use *when* as the includer. (§ 8.1)]

_____

_____

_____

7. Waterloo was a battle.
It decided the future of Europe for generations afterward.
[Make the second sentence into an adjectival clause modifying the noun *battle*. (§ 12.3)]

_____

_____

_____

8. The battle marked the end of Napoleon's career.
It signaled the end of French military domination of the continent.
[Rewrite these two sentences as one sentence with a compound predicate. (§ 7.2)]

_____

_____

_____

TASK B

1. Write two sentences that can be combined by making one an included adverbial clause that can be embedded in the other. (§ 8.1)

   The two sentences: _____

   _____

   The combined sentence: _____

   _____

2. Write two sentences with the same subject. Then make one into a half-sentence and embed it in the other. (§ 9.2–3)

   The two sentences: _____

   _____

   The one-and-a-half sentence: _____

   _____

3. Write a sentence with a compound predicate. Be sure that the second part of the predicate does not have its own subject. (§ 7.2)

   _____

   _____

4. Add either a front shifter or an end shifter to the sentence you wrote for 3 above. (§ 8.1)

   _____

   _____

5. First, complete the first sentence below by giving some identifying information about the subject. Then embed your sentence as an adjectival clause in the second one. (§ 12.3)

   The man _____

   The man got into an argument with a cab driver.

   _____

   _____

TASK C

Each pair of sentences that follows can be combined into a single effective sentence. Combine each pair, using one or another of the techniques discussed in Units 7–10. When you add an includer in order to embed one sentence in the other, try to choose the includer that best expresses the relation of the ideas.

1. Ancient Egypt was a matriarchal society.
   Daughters, rather than sons, inherited property.

   _____

   _____

2. The custom of female inheritance lasted a long time.
   The custom gave the women of Egypt considerable power.

   _____

   _____

3. Marriage contracts have survived.
   Marriage contracts show that women's rights were well respected.

   _____

   _____

4. The Egyptians were unlike some other cultures.
   The Egyptians did not consider marriage as being indissoluble.

   _____

   _____

5. A husband divorced his wife.
   He gave her back her dowry.

   _____

   _____

6. A man died.
   He left his wife a share of his property for the children.

   _____

   _____

7. The marriage failed.
   The husband or the wife could get a divorce easily.

   _____

   _____

8. The one desiring the divorce would pay the other a sum of money.
   The one desiring the divorce would say, "I divorce my husband (or wife)" to a group of witnesses.

   _____

   _____

TASK D

Write six or eight sentences about the position of women in our society today. Use the methods of sentence combining you have been working with to pack information into your sentences.

THE VERB KEY

The Base Form	The D-T-N Form	The ING Form	The Past Form	The Present Forms S Form	No-S Form
would, will		*was*	*(Yesterday)*	*(Every day)*	
should, shall		*were*	*(Last week)*	*(Twice a week)*	
could, can		*is*	*(A year ago)*	*(On Mondays)*	
might, may		*are*	*(etc.)*	*(Nowadays)*	
must		*am*		*(Now)*	
ought . . . (to)	*and also*	*and also*		*(etc.)*	
did, does, do	*having*	*having*	*I*	*it*	*I*
(or didn't,		*be*	*we*	*he*	*we*
doesn't, don't)		*been*	*you*	*she*	*you*
and to →		*being*¹	*it*		*they*
			he		
			she		
			they		
be	been	being	were/was	is	am/are
have	had	having	had	has	have
do	done	doing	did	does	do
break	broken	breaking	broke	breaks	break
go	gone	going	went	goes	go
get	got(ten)	getting	got	gets	get
eat	eaten	eating	ate	eats	eat
leave	left	leaving	left	leaves	leave
listen	listened	listening	listened	listens	listen
phone	phoned	phoning	phoned	phones	phone
read (=reed)	read (=red)	reading	read (=red)	reads	read (=reed)
say	said	saying	said	says	say
show	shown, showed	showing	showed	shows	show
sleep	slept	sleeping	slept	sleeps	sleep
tell	told	telling	told	tells	tell
wait	waited	waiting	waited	waits	wait
walk	walked	walking	walked	walks	walk

COMMON IRREGULAR VERBS

become	become	becoming	became	becomes	become
begin	begun	beginning	began	begins	begin
bring	brought	bringing	brought	brings	bring
buy	bought	buying	bought	buys	buy
choose	chosen	choosing	chose	chooses	choose
come	come	coming	came	comes	come
drive	driven	driving	drove	drives	drive
fall	fallen	falling	fell	falls	fall
find	found	finding	found	finds	find
fly	flown	flying	flew	flies	fly
give	given	giving	gave	gives	give
keep	kept	keeping	kept	keeps	keep
know	known	knowing	knew	knows	know
lie	lain	lying	lay	lies	lie
lose	lost	losing	lost	loses	lose
pay	paid	paying	paid	pays	pay
put	put	putting	put	puts	put
ride	ridden	riding	rode	rides	ride
rise	risen	rising	rose	rises	rise
see	seen	seeing	saw	sees	see
sit	sat	sitting	sat	sits	sit
speak	spoken	speaking	spoke	speaks	speak
think	thought	thinking	thought	thinks	think
take	taken	taking	took	takes	take
write	written	writing	wrote	writes	write

¹ The dotted arrow pointing from *being* to *had* shows that in passive sentences the verb forms that must follow *was, were, is, are, am, be, been,* or *being* are the D-T-N forms. In fact, every passive sentence must include some form of *to be* followed by some D-T-N form. The first sentence *has been done* for you. Everything we *were told* to do *has been done.* In fact, anything we *are ever told* to do *is always done.* That window *was broken* just last summer.

Some Common Includers

Adverbial	Nominal	Adjectival
after	how	after
although	if	as
as	that	before
because	what	such as
before	whatever	than
if	when	that
in case	where	till
now (that)	whether	until
once	which	when
since	whichever	where
so (that)	who	which
though	whoever	who
till	whom	whom
unless	whose	whose
until	why	
whatever		
when		
whenever		
whether		
while		